info@9marks.org | www.9marks.org

Tools like this are provided by the generous investment of donors.
Each gift to 9Marks helps equip church leaders with a biblical vision and practical resources for displaying God's glory to the nations through healthy churches.

Donate at: www.9marks.org/donate.

Or make checks payable to "9Marks" and mail to:
9 Marks
525 A St. NE
Washington, DC 20002

Editorial Director: Jonathan Leeman
Editor: Sam Emadi
Managing Editor: Alex Duke
Layout: Rubner Durais
Cover Design: OpenBox9
Production Manager: Rick Denham & Mary Beth Freeman
9Marks President: Mark Dever
Paperback: 978-1-955768-08-5
eBook: 978-1-955768-09-2

THE WHY OF ORDINARY MEANS OF GRACE MINISTRY

THE HOW OF ORDINARY MEANS OF GRACE MINISTRY

THE EFFECTS OF ORDINARY MEANS OF GRACE MINISTRY

Editor's Note:
Ordinary Means of Grace

Jonathan Leeman

For several years now, erstwhile 9Marks editor and now full-time pastor Sam Emadi, with a wink, has summarized our ministry, "Yeah, I just tell people, 9Marks exists to tell pastors not to do weird stuff. Just do what's in the Bible."

Not a bad summary.

If you've not heard the term "ordinary means of grace" before, Sam has captured what many pastors today need to hear: don't do weird stuff in your church. Don't take your growth cues from a marketing team. Don't lead church services that would make P. T. Barnum or J. J. Abrams proud. Don't, in short, think you can offer something extraordinary based on your creativity or ingenuity, or that you can manufacture the extraordinary through reverse-engineering the results you want.

The Spirit has already revealed everything we need for gathering and growing churches. And, yes, it's pretty ordinary stuff. You might even be tempted to call it boring and (ironically) uninspiring. Yet the uninspiring is inspired: preaching God's Word, singing God's Word, praying God's Word, reading God's Word, and declaring God's Word through the ordinances. Those ordinary—as opposed to extraordinary—practices have been ordained. The wisdom of God often sounds like foolishness, no?

Will preaching from this old book really change people? Will singing from it really transform our heart's affections? These are faith propositions. Believing in the power and effectiveness of the ordinary means requires faith. And too often we lack faith.

Oh, Lord, give us faith.

Very often pastors want extraordinary, and we reach for the extraordinary. We repeat William Carey's line about expecting and attempting great things for God. We want movements and revivals and explosive growth and immediacy. Alone in our offices, then, we get down on our knees, pound the floor, and beg God for a mass of conversions. "Save hundreds this week, Lord, even thousands."

I would not discourage you from praying that way. Those aren't wrong desires. But be careful not to let such prayers hide a sneaking faithlessness—the faithlessness of trying to live by sight rather than faith. How desperately we want to see the crowds turning to Christ with our eyes, to hear the wind of the Spirit moving with our ears, in order to know that our sacrifices have been worth it. Yet what if God asks you to labor for 40 years in front of 70 or 80 people at a time, three now leaving, four then coming, moving to another state, arriving from another city, with nothing sensational or Christian newsworthy happening the whole time, other than a dozen baptisms per year and all the signs of maturing saints learning to fight sin and love one another? Will you be content or feel a little dissatisfied?

Imagine then you arrive at Judgment Day, and the Lord replays the story of your life from his perspective. Week after week, you pounded the floor and asked God for the extraordinary. But then you got up off your knees and committed yourself once again to the ordinary means and only the ordinary means. You studied the Bible. You labored over your sermons. Then week after week you mounted the pulpit and commended yourself "by the open statement of the truth" (2 Cor. 4:2). Then, on this heavenly movie reel of your life, no movement began, no revival happened, but you watch as the several hundred people you ministered to in total over your pastorate raised godly children, shared the gospel with colleagues, and sent missionaries around the world. They in turn raised up thousands of disciples, both in your nation and around the world, who in turn raised up tens of thousands more; to say nothing of the hundreds of thousands and even millions of good deeds performed—wives encouraged, children nurtured, orphans adopted, disenfranchised employed, abused embraced, jobs created, and songs sung for the glory of God. What about now: will you still feel a little dissatisfied? Or will your jaw drop at the wonder of the Lord using you—sinful and inconsistent ole YOU!—to bear such fruit?

We fixate on the ocean surface, yet the real action is in the unseen currents below.

A member of my church recently asked me what the main "enemy" 9Marks is working against. I could have answered by pointing to sin or various worldly philosophies. I said "pragmatism." But that word isn't actually big enough to capture what I meant. So I further explained there are two main paths evangelical pastors take in ministry—the path of revival or the path of revivalism, the First Great Awakening or the Second Great Awakening, relying on God's ingenuity or relying on our own, relying on the Spirit or relying on the psychology and sociology of movements, the path of faith or the path of sight, the ordinary means of grace or pragmatism.

With all this in mind, you might say this Journal, which focuses on the ordinary means of grace, presents the very heart of the 9Marks church program. What's our church model? Here it is.

Don’t Do Weird Stuff

Sam Emadi

“So you work for 9Marks, huh? Aren’t their views on church kind of radical?”

I’d been here before but still didn’t quite know where to take this awkward conversation. Explain why I think New Testament polity is prescriptive? Nope, too heady. Show how the Reformers advocated these same doctrines? Nope, too geeky. I opted for something much simpler.

“We’re not radical,” I said, “we basically just encourage churches: ‘*Hey, don’t do weird stuff.*’”

THE WEIRD STUFF WE DO

Churches do lots of weird things. Some of that weirdness is a bit outlandish. A few years ago, a pastor in eastern Kentucky decided that traditional “baptismal waters” were a little too tame for his taste, so he started dunking new converts in pools of beer. In God’s providence, while writing this very paragraph, a friend sent me a YouTube clip of a preacher instructing his congregation to take their socks off and wave them over their heads while he improvised a song about how Jesus is spinning them “around … right round.”

Of course, most pastors and churches are sensible enough to avoid such ostentatious displays of weirdness. But we’ve got plenty of well-intentioned, respectable weirdness to go around. We've abandoned congregational singing for stage performers. We claim to be a people of the cross, but design our services around triumphalism, prosperity, and unbroken jolly-ness. We crave "worship" that serves up sentimentality rather than our need to repent and believe the gospel.

Most evangelical churches in America still have at their core the profound and simple elements of worship modeled by the early church: "And they devoted themselves to the apostles' teaching and the fellowship, to the breaking of bread and the prayers" (Acts 2:42). Yet in many churches these simple acts of worship have been encrusted over by years of accumulated traditions that mask the beautiful simplicity of the ordinary means of grace.

WHY WE DO WEIRD STUFF

Why have churches strayed from the ordinary means of grace and the simplicity of apostolic worship represented in Acts 2:42. Here are a few reasons.

1. We've lost our appetite for God's majesty.

David Wells notes in his book *God in the Wasteland:*

> The fundamental problem in the evangelical world today is not inadequate technique, insufficient organization, or antiquated music; and those who want to squander the church's resources bandaging these scratches will do nothing to stanch the flow of blood that is spilling from its true wounds. The fundamental problem in the evangelical world today is that God rests too inconsequentially upon the church. His truth is too distant, his grace is too ordinary, his judgment is too benign, his gospel is too easy, and his Christ is too common. (30)

The ordinary means of grace challenge our self-obsession and relentless pursuit of positive emotional fulfillment. They fixate our attention with laser-like focus on the majesty of God—majesty that both delights and terrifies. It forces our worship into a posture of "reverence and awe, for our God is a consuming fire (Heb. 12:28–29).

2. We've lost our appetite for ecclesiology.

Churches often deviate from the ordinary means of grace simply because they've never considered that ecclesiology shapes ministry, even down to what we do on Sunday mornings. God hasn't authorized us to devise our corporate worship services or our ministry according to our tastes. Instead, he's said that what we *do* in worship should represent who we *are* as a church.

3. We've cultivated an appetite for entertainment and "positive emotions."

The ordinary means of grace are aptly named—they're ordinary. There's nothing flashy or enticing about them. In a world of Marvel-sized spectacles, it's easy to get insecure that the ordinary means simply won't cut it. Furthermore, the ordinary means of grace resist our attempts to engineer certain emotional responses from the congregation. After all, it's rather easy apart from the ordinary means of grace to design a service that produces a particular emotional response from the congregation.

But the ordinary means of grace put ourselves in a place of submission to God's purposes for the congregation—purposes which sometimes include lament for sin, grief over loss, or solemnity at the cost of discipleship.

HOW TO STOP BEING WEIRD

At the heart of these diagnoses is the fact that much of the church has embraced the world's perspective on the cross—we consider it foolishness. But the ordinary means of grace embrace the folly of the cross; they place it front and center in all that we do.

Embracing the ordinary means of grace as a sufficient and comprehensive approach to ministry isn't merely about coming to the right theological conclusions, it's a matter of the heart. Do we *really* trust God to work through the simple means he has ordained, or do we believe our ingenuity supplies something the ordinary means lack?

In Scripture, attempts to "help God out" generally turn sideways.

Just ask Abraham and Sarah how their masterplan to obtain a seed through Hagar worked out. They learned the hard way that "that which is born of the flesh is flesh, and that which is born of the Spirit is spirit" (John 3:6). Too often, we think we can produce spiritual fruit outside the ordinary means of grace. But we can only make Ishmaels; God alone makes Isaacs.

For years, 9Marks has been standing with historic Protestantism advocating the ordinary means of grace. There's nothing radical about this proposal. In fact, it's squarely in line with the central Protestant conviction that we relate to God by faith and by faith alone. When we give ourselves to the simplicity of apostolic worship and the ordinary means of grace, we live by faith, *trusting* that God will accomplish what he's promised to accomplish—and he'll do so in a way that ensures he gets the credit, not us. So don't do weird stuff. God acts in the ordinary.

ABOUT THE AUTHOR

Sam Emadi is the Senior Pastor at Hunsinger Lane Baptist Church in Louisville, KY and serves as the Senior Editor at 9Marks.

Do Weird Stuff

Alex Duke

Before I graduated college, I'd witnessed the following things in church:

It was my childhood pastor's 40th anniversary. To celebrate, they bought him a gift: a brand-new, white-as-a-pearl Toyota Avalon. Though they couldn't find a way to get the car on stage, they did find a way to show a live feed of it pulling up to the church, much to our pastor's surprise. It felt like a Showcase Showdown sans Bob Barker.

It was Super Bowl Sunday, 2008. The pastors of my church in college dressed up as the two opposing quarterbacks—Eli Manning and Tom Brady—and honestly, I don't remember much after that. But football featured prominently.

It was a summer Lord's Day in Brooklyn, probably 2009 or 2010. Between the songs and the sermon, a church member, in order to exercise his "gift," delivered a comedy set. I remember laughing more than once.

It was Father's Day. A gifted singer who sounded like George Strait sang a solo about fatherhood. It was Mother's Day. A gifted singer who sounded like Kelly Clarkson sang a solo about motherhood. The moms in attendance all received roses. It was Memorial Day. A gifted choir who sounded like a gifted choir sang about valor and sacrifice.

I could keep going. I could talk about the awkward skits or the time a camel walked down the aisle or the sermon series on movies or singing the national anthem or the white-gloved handbell choir or the performative dances—twirlers and all.

I'd witnessed all these things in church. And you know what? Precisely none of them were weird to me. It was all as normal as the sunrise, as ordinary as a butter knife.

Until it wasn't.

"IS THIS PLACE CRAZY?"

It was January 2013. Through God's strange and hilarious providence I'd ended up literally in Mark Dever's backyard. In other words, I'd started an internship at Capitol Hill Baptist Church having never before attended Capitol Hill Baptist Church or a church even kind of like Capitol Hill Baptist Church. I'd become Reformed or Calvinist or whatever through the preaching I heard in college, but I basically had no idea what a church was.

Nonetheless, I shuffled into the PAC-MAN–shaped auditorium and sat next to my wife. We were 23 years old and recently married.

Here's the rundown of that morning's service. Try to read it out-loud without taking a breath:

Three "prep songs" while people found their seats

- Welcome and announcements
- A call to worship
- Three more hymns
- A prayer of praise (around 5 minutes)
- A Scripture reading from the Old Testament
- Another hymn
- A Scripture reading from the New Testament
- A pastoral prayer of petition (around 10 minutes)
- Another hymn
- A prayer of thanks (around 1 minute)
- The offering
- The sermon (around 55 minutes)
- A hymn
- A celebration of the Lord's Supper (around 15 minutes)
- Two more hymns
- A benediction
- A brief time of reflections and preparation

No, no. Don't skip it. Seriously, read through that list. It's like The Cheesecake Factory's menu. It has everything but baptism.

By the end of this gathering—which lasted a cruel-and-unusual two and a half hours—I felt exhausted, emaciated, and a little bit enraptured. I was also antsy about my fantasy football team. Somehow, the 1PM NFL games were about to start!

Interns had a job after church: to stand by the exits as people left. I stood there, wide-eyed and bushy-tailed. I shook hand after hand and returned smile after smile. "Thank you for coming," I said. But I wanted to say something else: "Is this place crazy? Are you crazy? Am I crazy?"

For 23 years, I'd gone to church every Sunday of my life. But I'd never seen anything like that first Lord's Day in 2013. It was weird.

Until it wasn't.

The next five months were a whirlwind. At first, the experience measured out as equal parts curious, confounding, and captivating. But over time, as I sat through service planning meetings and heard the rationale behind every—yes, every—decision, I began to understand some things. Many curiosities remained—what's a "potentate"? do we really need that many separate prayers? does Mark really need to preach that long? But by the end of my time on the Hill, what had confounded me largely faded away and the whole thing began to click.

DO WEIRD STUFF

My friend Sam Emadi wrote a piece in this Journal called "Don't Do Weird Stuff." It's good. You should read it. He talks about funny things like baptizing people in beer. The goal of this piece is to make the same point from the opposite perspective. I want to encourage you to do weird stuff. Stuff that won't make much sense to the majority of rank-and-file churchgoers, stuff that won't make immediate sense to people who don't know Jesus and never think about God, stuff that seekers won't be sensitive toward.

I'm not encouraging weirdness for weirdness' sake. I'm not celebrating churches that are arcane, inscrutable, and, to borrow a word from Andy Dufresne, "obtuse." I'm simply encouraging you to make sure the bullseye of every gathering is orderly edification and intelligible instruction that leads saints to worship the God they adore. That's Paul's bullseye in 1 Corinthians 14.

Some might say this emphasis erodes evangelism. Quite the opposite actually. A Christian gathering shouldn't leave the unbeliever primarily saying to themselves, "Wow, I'm really welcome here among you," but rather, "Wow, God really is among you" (1 Cor. 14:20).

And for that to happen, I'm convinced we'll have to do some weird stuff. We'll have to talk about God a lot. We'll have to talk to God a lot. We'll have to place his Word on a pedestal, not the periphery. We'll have to accentuate the stark differences between Christianity and everything else even as we acknowledge the essential similarities between Christians and everyone else made.

Must it look like Capitol Hill Baptist Church? Of course not. Must it take two-and-a-half hours? No way. Must it sing about "potentates" and "rolling spheres" and being "ineffably sublime"? Absolutely. (I'm just kidding.)

I've heard Mark say something before like, "Pray so much in your gatherings that the people who only pretend to love Jesus will get bored." He's on to something. But there's more to say. Because while some will be bored to death, others will get their first whiff of true life (2 Cor. 2:16).

ABOUT THE AUTHOR

Alex Duke is the editorial manager of 9Marks. He lives in Louisville, Kentucky, where he also works at Third Avenue Baptist Church as the Director of Youth Ministry and Ecclesiological Training.

Liturgies Are the Pipes, But the Word Is the Water

Matt McCullough

Over the past decade or so, I've been grateful for the surge of interest in liturgy in my little circle of evangelicalism.

I know the term itself can be a little slippery. I've seen it applied to everything from an ancient prayer book to your morning coffee routine. But where it refers to an intentional structure for our weekly gatherings, liturgy captures something that ought to be precious to all of us.

Whether we recognize it or not, all of our gatherings have a liturgy. Our corporate liturgies affect us, and none of them is neutral. We're shaped by what we regularly do in powerful ways we may not recognize. So much the wiser, then, to be intentional about what we're doing and why. We must be careful to aim our service order at what will honor God and encourage each other.

But in our embrace of liturgy, there's also a danger to avoid. Liturgies are tools we develop and deploy. Whether we draw them from an ancient sourcebook or build them in weekly staff meetings, we must realize that the order of our gathering is a strategy that we've decided is best. We have to guard against the assumption that the key to effective formation of people is what *we* bring to the table.

To put it positively, we have to make sure our hope and confidence for Christian formation rests on the power of God's Word backed by God's Spirit—from the miracle of the new birth through the lifelong process of sanctification.

"Faith comes from hearing," Paul says in Romans 10, "and hearing through the Word of Christ."

"Having begun by the Spirit," Paul says in Galatians 3, "are you now being perfected by the flesh?"

From beginning to end, our formation depends on God's power at work in us. He works in us by his Word. Good liturgy is merely the delivery system for this miraculous power to save. It's the piping that carries the life-giving water. It's the trellis that holds up the fruit-bearing vine.

So here's the key question: in our use of liturgy, how can we make sure our confidence is in the power of God's Word, not the creativity or ingenuity of our methods?

Here are three questions to ask.

FIRST, IS YOUR LITURGY SATURATED WITH THE BIBLE?

Make sure you're drawn to more than the gravitas that comes with age and formality, or the transcendence that comes through terms rarely used in common speech. What makes a guide like the *Book of Common Prayer* so useful is not how old it is or how consistently beautiful its language may be, but the fact that Cranmer filled these forms with Scripture. Does your liturgy make room for lots of Bible reading? Are your prayers regularly responding to what the Bible says? Do your songs draw heavily from the language of Scripture?

SECOND, IS YOUR LITURGY SHAPED BY THE STORY OF THE BIBLE?

The Bible isn't an encyclopedia. It's a love story. It explains why we exist, where all this beauty comes from, what's gone wrong and what we can hope for. Through many twists and turns, it tells a story about the God who made everything and the people he made in his image. Our liturgies show confidence in God's Word when they take on the shape of God's Word. We want to make sure they account for creation, fall, redemption, and restoration.

That means we should make sure our gatherings praise God for the beauty of his character—for who he is as God. We need regular confession of sin that prepares us for the assurance of the gospel. We need to give thanks for that good news. We need prayers of supplication that treat God as a Father who loves to give good gifts to his children. And we want to listen to his Word for the perspective and hope we can't get anywhere else.

FINALLY, IS YOUR LITURGY CENTERED ON PREACHING FROM THE BIBLE?

My impression is that renewed enthusiasm for liturgy sometimes comes with a devaluation of the sermon in our gatherings.

The argument goes something like this. Protestants have overemphasized the importance of verbal communication. This creates malformed, bobble-head Christians, with minds full of knowledge but everyday lives that are too often unaffected. Their lives remain unaffected because embodied people need more than new ideas to experience change. They need new habits. They need embodied practices that work at a subconscious level to aim our desires in new directions. If we want to form people, then we have to account for how people work and choose our strategies accordingly.

I see more of my own imbalance in that critique of word-centered Protestantism than I'd like to admit. I know I've got a lot to learn about the value of habits in the process of sanctification.

But here's my central concern with this argument: our commitment to biblical preaching has never been based on what makes people tick. It's not a strategy that flows from anthropological insight. We don't assume that people are best formed by 40-minute talks that move ideas from one mind to another.

We don't build our strategies with anthropology any more than Joshua, at the walls of Jericho, built his strategy with structural engineering. We preach Christ in all the Scriptures for the same reason they circled that city and then blew their horns. Not because this is supposed to work, but because God promised that it would. This method isn't ours. It's his. "Preach the word; be ready in season and out of season" (2 Timothy 4:2).

We prioritize preaching because we trust the Word. It's the sword of God's Spirit, two-edged and piercing, living and active, reaching beneath the surface and all the way down to the marrow of the soul. We know people aren't hard-wired for formation by what passes through their ears and into their minds. But this is entirely beside the point. Old, childless men don't normally father nations. Small young men don't normally slay giants. Crucified men don't normally bring life to the dead. The fact that biblical preaching shouldn't be expected to produce heart change is part of why God chose this delivery system for the work he's doing in our lives. He loves to confound our expectations. He loves to show his strength in our weakness. Or, as Paul puts it in 1 Corinthians, it pleases God "through the folly of what we preach to save those who believe." Why? "So that your faith might not rest in the wisdom of men but in the power of God" (1 Corin 1:21, 2:5).

When we start with people and build our strategies on what we've learned about them, the pressure to get through to them rests on our shoulders. If we're successful, the glory stays with us, too. But when we start with what God has said, even something so foolish as the preaching of the cross, he gets the glory when Christians take on the image of his Son. And what we get is freedom—the freedom to do as we're told and to watch as he works.

ABOUT THE AUTHOR

Matt McCullough is the pastor of Trinity Church in Nashville, Tennessee.

Why the Ordinary Means of Grace Must Be Central in Our Gatherings

David Strain

The Westminster Shorter Catechism provides as helpful a definition as any of the means of grace:

> The outward and ordinary means whereby Christ communicates to us the benefits of redemption are his ordinances, especially the Word, sacraments and prayer; all which are made effectual to the elect for salvation. (Question 88)

All the ordinances of God, but especially the Word read and preached, the sacraments of baptism and the Supper, and the prayers of the people of God: these are the outward and ordinary means Christ uses to impart the blessings of the gospel to his people by the Holy Spirit. And I daresay that every evangelical would agree that these are the constituent elements of Christian worship, commanded by Scripture, and normative for the church.

To be sure, some of us might quibble over the language here or there. Some dislike the word "sacraments." Some worry that calling these ordinances of God "means of grace" might convey the mistaken idea that simply in the performance of these outward acts grace is conferred (which is not at all what the phrase intends). But these differences aside, the Word of God read and preached, prayed and sung, seen in baptism and tasted in the Lord's Supper—all agree that these are the fundamentals of Christian worship. They are the primary mechanisms given to us for our discipleship. So far, so good.

It remains, however, a perennially pressing question as to what role these elements ought to play in any given Sunday service. Certainly, they ought to feature regularly in the life of the church. But can't we do other things too? Can't we set aside some part or other of these ordinary means, in favor of something special once in a while?

Perhaps the simplest way to respond to these challenges is to parse the phrase "ordinary means of grace."

1. ORDINARY MEANS ORDAINED.

Calling the means of grace "ordinary" teaches us two things. First, these means are appointed. They are "ordinary," in the sense of having been *ordained* by God in Holy Scripture. That's why the catechism calls them "ordinances." The classic text for this assertion is Acts 2:42, where we read of the post-Pentecostal church that "they devoted themselves to the apostles' teaching and the fellowship, to the breaking of bread and the prayers."

When we ask what Christians should do when they gather in churches on the first day of the week, Scripture has answers for us: reading the Bible, preaching the gospel, praying, singing, and observing baptism and the Supper. That's what we should do. That's it. When Paul wrote to Timothy, to encourage him in his new pastorate at Ephesus, his Ministry 101 refresher course is remarkably clear. As contemporary evangelicals, we are often prone to measuring church vitality by the Three Bs: buildings, bodies, and budgets. That's how we know things are going well. But Paul wants Timothy focused elsewhere.

Listen to his counsel to the young pastor:

> I charge you in the presence of God and of Christ Jesus, who is to judge the living and the dead, and by his appearing and his kingdom: [2] preach the word; be ready in season and out of season; reprove, rebuke, and exhort, with complete patience and teaching. [3] For the time is coming when people will not endure sound teaching, but having itching ears they will accumulate for themselves teachers to suit their own passions, [4] and will turn away from listening to the truth and wander off into myths. [5] As for you, always be sober-minded, endure suffering, do the work of an evangelist, fulfill your ministry. (2 Timothy 4:1–5)

Timothy faces mounting pressure to give people what they prefer, what sits more easily with them, what they enjoy. Paul presses him in the opposite direction. He tells Timothy to remain resolute in giving people what they *need*. In other words, he needs to preach the Word. The central means appointed by God for the gathering-in of the lost and the growing-up of the found is the preaching of the Word. It's not flashy. It's not novel. But it is what God has ordained.

So pastors, just do that. It might be harder (notice that Timothy is to "endure suffering" as he does the "work of an evangelist"!). It might result in slower measurable growth in your buildings, bodies, and budgets. But it is God's way, so it must be ours.

2. ORDINARY MEANS *NOT* EXTRAORDINARY.

Secondly, the word ordinary needs to be set in contrast to its antonym: *extraordinary*. To be sure, God regularly made use of many extraordinary means to impart his grace to his people. All of the miracles and revelatory gifts were extraordinary. And fidelity to Scripture compels us to maintain that God remains free to work as he wills.

But surely, we ought never to neglect the *ordinary* means while we look expectantly for him to work through the *extraordinary*. The context of Acts 2:42 is once again important here. If ever there was an unusual and extraordinary season in the life of the church, this was it. But what characterizes the newly Spirit-empowered church in the grip of what we might today recognize as a remarkable revival? Well, it's *not* an obsession with the new and the unusual and the innovative and the extraordinary. No, the church is devoted to the Word, the sacraments, and prayer. There is not chaos. There is clarity. The Word of God was mighty in their midst and the people responded in prayer and praise. There is no smoke and mirrors, no gimmicks or pizazz, no central personality or rock-star leader. The Word did the work.

3. REMEMBER: THEY ARE A MEANS OF *GRACE*.

Finally, we need to remember that our worship services ought to focus on the ordinary means of grace not only because they are *ordinary*, but also because they are a means of *grace*. In my judgment, the best way to understand how the Word, the sacraments, and prayer communicate to us the saving grace of Christ, is to focus on the way the Word works. Hebrews 4:2 speaks of the fathers of Israel who derived no benefit from the Word preached because it was "unmixed with faith" or, as some versions have it, because they were not joined by faith to those who believed the Word. Either way, the point is the same: benefitting from the Word requires faith. Faith takes hold of the grace on offer in the Word.

The sacraments are "visible words," as Calvin said, echoing Augustine. And they work in the same way. We receive them, believing the gospel they depict—and by believing, we receive the grace they offer. Similarly, prayer takes God at his promise and offers up "our desires unto God for things agreeable to his Word" (Westminster Shorter Catechism 98). Prayer is a pleading of the promises of the Word back to God. But the *Word* is the main thing.

And when we put the main thing at the heart of all we do, we put ourselves on the road toward blessing, toward the grace of God in Jesus Christ. So why would we look elsewhere when we know that God has promised to meet us here, in the Word, in the sacraments, and in prayer?

So then, when we gather, let's not mess around with our own homespun techniques. In faith, let us read the Word, preach the Word, pray the Word, sing the Word, and see and taste and touch the Word. As we do, surely the grace promised in the Word will be ours to the glory of the Triune God.

ABOUT THE AUTHOR

Rev. David Strain is senior minister of the First Presbyterian Church in Jackson, Miss., and chairman of the board of Christian Witness to Israel (North America).

Why Preaching Is Primary and the Ordinances Aren't

Jonty Rhodes

One Passover in the first half of the first century, a traveler watches from a distance as three men are crucified on a hill outside Jerusalem. What does he learn? His eyes will tell him little. Other than some unusual weather patterns and a quicker-than-usual death in the case of one of the men, all he notices are a few ordinary-looking Jewish men being executed by Rome.

But once he comes within earshot, everything changes. Amongst other things he hears the crucified men talking. One admits his guilt and asks the central figure, apparently called "Jesus," to remember him when he comes into his kingdom. He hears this Jesus promise that the criminal will that very day enter paradise. He also hears the centurion overseeing the crucifixion declare that Jesus was "the Son of God." After a while, he hears Jesus announce that his work is "finished," and then he commits his spirit to his heavenly Father.

Though the traveler's eyes alone taught him little, his ears have opened the door of salvation. As it was with our fictional traveler, so it is with us today.

"Faith comes from hearing, and hearing through the word of Christ" (Rom. 10:17).

WHAT ABOUT THE ORDINANCES?

In his kindness, Jesus gave us two ordinances—two pictures of the gospel—in baptism and the Lord's Supper. Both are vital to a healthy church. To ignore either would be to ignore Jesus. But the preaching of the Word of God must always have priority over the ordinances. Why? Because signs only have meaning when accompanied by words which explain them. I've heard that in the earliest days of British radio broadcasting, the BBC came to an agreement with the newspapers that they wouldn't undermine sales by commentating on horse-racing. So instead they played the sound of the race—hooves thundering, crowds cheering—with no words to explain what was happening. It sounds so ridiculous it might well be true.

But a worship service that ignored the preaching of the gospel, and instead put all the attention on baptism or the Lord's Supper would be far more foolish. Let's look at just three reasons why this is so.

THE EXAMPLE OF PAUL

"For Christ did not send me to baptize but to preach the gospel" (1 Cor. 1:17).

Paul certainly baptized people, though at times he seems to have forgotten quite whom (1 Cor 1:16). But he clearly believed his central task was preaching Christ crucified. By the time we get to the book of Acts, we hear little of the Lord's Supper. But we see Paul preaching at nearly every opportunity.

When the divisions in the early church threatened to overwhelm the other apostles, they decided, "It is not right that we should give up preaching the word of God to serve tables" (Acts 6:2), and resolved instead to "devote ourselves to prayer and to the ministry of the word" (Acts 6:4). Prayerful preaching of the

Word was the clear priority of the earliest church leaders.

THE INSTRUCTION OF PAUL

As Paul looked to a future when the church would be without apostles, led instead by "ordinary" men such as Timothy and Titus, he concerned himself again with faithful preaching. He told Timothy, "Devote yourself to the public reading of Scripture, to exhortation, to teaching" (1 Tim 4:13). He reminded Titus that God had manifested the gospel "in his word through the preaching with which I have been entrusted by the command of God our Savior" (Titus 1:3). No wonder that some of Paul's final words are also some of his weightiest:

"I charge you in the presence of God and of Christ Jesus, who is to judge the living and the dead, and by his appearing and his kingdom: preach the word; be ready in season and out of season; reprove, rebuke, and exhort, with complete patience and teaching" (2 Tim. 4:1–2).

The pastoral epistles have few, if any, references to the ordinances. But the command to preach rings through each.

THE EXAMPLE OF JESUS

Of course, Paul and Timothy were only following in their Master's footsteps. He put a high premium on his preaching ministry. When the crowds of Capernaum came flocking for healing, having seen Jesus's power over disease and demon alike, Christ told Simon it was necessary instead "to go on to the next towns, that I may preach there also, for that is what I came for" (Mk. 1:38).

Why did Jesus leave the good work of healing in order to preach to new flocks? Because he was the Sower, who's word bore fruit and unlocked entry to the eternal kingdom (Mk. 4:1–20).

Still today it is through the Word, not the bare ordinances, that men and women are "born again, not of perishable seed but of imperishable, through the living and abiding word of God" (1 Pet. 1:23). It is the Word read and preached that is able to convert the sceptic and disciple the saint (2 Tim. 3:15–17). Ordinances without

Word will save no one, whereas the Word without the ordinances has saved many.

We mustn't ignore the ordinances. But let's keep the sermon central.

ABOUT THE AUTHOR

Jonty Rhodes is the founding pastor of Christ Church Central (IPC) in Leeds, England.

How Programs Fit into an Ordinary Means of Grace Ministry

Mike McKinley

When we speak of "ordinary means of grace" ministry, we are really talking about ministry that is built on a foundation of confidence in God's sovereignty. If the fruitfulness of our congregations depends on our skill, effort, and cleverness, then our efforts will be best invested in coming up with programs and strategies that are most likely to bring about the desired results. But we know from the Bible that *God* is the one "who gives the growth" (1 Cor. 3:6) and that salvation "depends not on human will or exertion, but on God, who has mercy" (Romans 9:16). As a result, the question that ought to shape our approach to ministry is this: what sort of activities has God freely and sovereignly commanded and promised to bless? That is to say, through what means does he work in order to draw, strengthen, encourage, build up, mature, and capture the hearts of his people?

We might use a handful of different words to indicate these activities, but they boil down to a few ideas:

- God calls and blesses his people through his Word, especially when it is preached, but also when it is read in private or in smaller groups.
- God gives grace in response to the prayers of his people, whether they are offered in corporate settings, in small groups, or in private.
- God blesses his people through the sacraments (baptism and the Lord's Supper). When God's people come in faith to be baptized or to the Table, they experience communion with him and each other and the strengthening of their faith and joy in the Lord.
- God also shapes and edifies his people through the local church, particularly its fellowship, care, oversight, and discipline.

Now, those four means of grace might not seem like much in terms of an effective ministry strategy. It seems like a church would need much more than just those ordinary activities in order to grow in size and maturity. It seems obvious that it would be more effective for a church to create a series of carefully targeted programs aimed at generating interest, excitement, and involvement. This is why so many churches seem to spend so much of their time and energy on putting together bigger and better programs, things like:

- Camps for children and youth
- Big holiday gatherings (Trunk or Treat, anyone?) for the community
- Meetings aimed at people with specific needs (recovery, grief, singleness, divorce)
- Events designed to get men or women together

But God has always had a way of doing things that confounds our expectations in order to magnify and glorify his wisdom (1 Cor. 1:18–31). So a church that trusts in God's sovereign power to save and build his church will focus on those ordinary means of grace more than a series of splashy programs.

But that doesn't mean that there's no room for programs in the life of a healthy church. In fact, as long as they occupy the proper place, programs can help people to grow in Christ and experience his grace. But the tricky part is that phrase "the proper place." What is the proper place for programs?

Here's the key: **our programs are helpful only to the extent that they put people in contact with the God-ordained means of grace**. It doesn't matter if a program draws a crowd of unsaved or unchurched people; it doesn't matter if it's well-attended by church members. Many programs create the *appearance* of growth and progress without actually seeing much of the Lord's work accomplished.

What matters is that we engage people with the means of grace. If God saves people through their hearing his proclaimed Word (Romans 10:17), then we want our outreach programs to create opportunities for unbelievers to hear the gospel Word. If God causes his people to grow through his Word, then we want our children's programs, our youth programs, and our adult discipleship programs to be focused around God's Word. If God blesses his people in response to their prayers, then we want to design our programs to encourage the church to pray. If God uses the fellowship of the saints and the oversight of a church's elders as a means of grace, then we want our programs to facilitate those relationships.

Here are a few examples of programs that serve an "ordinary means of grace" ministry model:

- A food distribution and community garden brings our neighbors onto our church's campus, where church members can meet them, build relationships with them, pray for them, and invite them to read the Bible.
- A Bible study for at-risk youth gives them a chance to hang out in a loving home, have a good meal, play some games, and study the Bible.
- An after-school homework club helps immigrant children with their homework and teaches them the Bible.

- Church members are set up with one another for one-to-one Bible reading, where they use study notes prepared by one of the elders.
- A men's group meets to read a Christian book and break up into small groups to talk about their lives and pray together.

These programs serve the larger purpose of exposing people to the things that God has said he will use to bless his people. This approach to ministry requires church leaders to regularly evaluate these activities to make sure they're actually serving their intended purpose. Without regular evaluation, programs tend to become ends unto themselves, and well-intentioned Christians can sometimes see their role in the church as continuing certain ministries, even when they're no longer effective. In order to deploy programs well, church leaders need to be able to explain how a certain program exposes people to the means of grace, and then be very honest in evaluating whether or not it's actually accomplishing its purpose.

ABOUT THE AUTHOR
Mike is an author and the pastor of Sterling Park Baptist Church in Sterling, Virginia.

How A Good Desire for Church Growth Can Lead to Bad Ministry Practices

Harshit Singh

THE WORLDWIDE PROBLEM

Many pastors around the world are weighed down with a heavy burden to see numerical growth. Whether you pastor in the global West or the East, you can feel the pressure.

Sometimes the desire for numerical growth is good-natured. A pastor wants to reach more lost people and provide faithful teaching to more people. Sometimes the desire is for pragmatic reasons. More people will make the church more financially viable, a pastor reasons. And a bigger budget can accomplish more ministry. And sometimes the desire for numerical growth is compromised. A man lusts for greater personal influence. Or to impress his donors and raise more support. Or to take pride in leading a large church.

The desire for numeric growth, in turn, leads many pastors to constantly look for growth strategies.

THE WRONG PATH

The trouble is this preoccupation with numbers sets us as pastors on the wrong trajectory. It lures us away from our primary calling of faithfully shepherding the flock that God has entrusted to us.

Let me assume for a second, pastor, that you desire such growth. What happens when you *don't* see hordes of people thronging through the church doors? When your dreams don't match reality are you tempted to think you're doing something wrong? Or that you're failing to do something you should do?

When such thoughts come, hopefully you turn to the Scriptures. But sadly, it's all too easy for us to look elsewhere. We can turn to other churches that seem to enjoy the growth we desire. We read books and attend seminars that celebrate all kinds of strategies. Perhaps we begin to focus on understanding the culture around us. We take polls and surveys to figure out what our neighbors might connect with. We assume the survey answers will help us know what people are really looking for and how we can connect our church to those needs.

I've spent a few years in the global West. I watched as pastors were tempted to think just the right kind of music or the right kind of programs or the right kind of application in preaching would do the trick. Pastoring in the East, as I do, I've watched as pastors feel the temptation to offer promises of healing, exorcism, or prosperity. But no matter where you are or what packages of promises tempt us, such philosophies of ministry address felt needs. They appeal to the flesh, soften the offence of the gospel, and sugarcoat its demands.

Yet here's what escapes our attention when we build our churches on these kinds of "attractional" strategies: we risk building on something other than the cross of Christ and the gospel. We also fail our people when we don't warn them that they will pay a price to follow Christ.

Worse still, you can cajole people into making decisions based on false promises of breakthroughs, a renewed purpose in life, a perfect loving community, prosperity, freedom from harm, even utopia! Sometimes the lies are blatant; more often they are subtle and disguised.

In the process, you offer a different Christ to people, one who appeals to their natural and often selfish desires, but who doesn't confront their sin, demand repentance, and command total submission in all areas of their lives. Maybe they even join your church, but it's not because they want a crucified Christ. They certainly don't want to deny themselves and carry their cross to follow him.

Brother pastor, if you can see yourself in this at all, I appeal to you for love's sake, be careful. My guess is you might assume that, if lots of people are showing up, it must be the work of the Spirit. You tell yourself, as long as the lost are reached, it doesn't matter what strategy is being employed. But that's not true. The Spirit isn't the only one who can draw a crowd.

I can understand the impulse to lovingly disarm people, help them be comfortable, meet them where they are, and be relevant. I understand how you can tell yourself, "Let's just make first contact, and offer an easy introduction to the spiritual journey. Once the seekers have taken the first few steps, then we'll present Christ's demands." But ask yourself, did Jesus adopt this method? Is there any risk of bait-and-switch?

When you begin by promising people what they want, it's difficult to follow up with Christ's demands. If you do preach them to the church, folk respond with disillusionment, disappointment, and departure. Those who do stick around do so as long as they can get what they first came for: healing, wealth, prosperity, kids' programs, community, music, and so forth.

I trust you heard the phrase, what you win them with, you win them to. That's a real problem. When we build our churches by trying to attract people with what we know they like, we continually risk affirming people in the self-centeredness and consumerism. Some people will become Christians, but they won't grow, remaining spiritual dwarfs. The crowd on the whole, furthermore, will prove not to have loyalty or commitment. They'll be fickle, hard to please, easily disappointed. The day some other church can offer them something more exciting, more thrilling, they will be out of the door.

In the meantime, your pastoral team will practically kill themselves trying every trick to stay afloat in the market and retain an edge over your competitors. And, brother pastor, I don't want any of this for you.

THE WONDERFUL PANACEA

Consider Paul's strategy instead. You might find it refreshing. And simple. He writes,

> And I, when I came to you, brothers, did not come proclaiming to you the testimony of God with lofty speech or wisdom. For I decided to know nothing among you except Jesus Christ and him crucified. And I was with you in weakness and in fear and much trembling, and my speech and my message were not in plausible words of wisdom, but in demonstration of the Spirit and of power, so that your faith might not rest in the wisdom of men but in the power of God. (1 Corinthians 2:1–5)

Paul did not want to draw people with the wisdom of men. He wanted the faith of his hearers to rest in the power of God and nothing else. That's why he was simply going to preach the gospel of Christ crucified.

This is exactly what we must do. When we preach this gospel, his sheep hear his voice—and they come to him, not to *us*, but to him! They don't have to be lured or pampered or coerced. They come because they see Christ's glory, and they stay because they love Christ's glory. As long as they hear his voice and see his glory in the preaching of the gospel, they will stay.

I'm reminded of what Simon Peter said to Jesus: "Lord, to whom shall we go? You have the words of eternal life" (John 6:68). It really is as simple as that. Once people see Jesus, then Jesus and his words are enough. Enough to draw them, enough to keep them, enough to sustain them, enough to bring them home!

ABOUT THE AUTHOR

Harshit Singh is the pastor of Zion Church in Lucknow, India.

Good News, Ordinary Pastor! You Don't Need a Winning Personality

Dan Miller

All men are created equal. No two men are equally created. On one hand, all people are created in God's image and every believer enjoys full status as God's adopted child in union with Christ. On the other hand, our sovereign Creator employs a single-use template of individuality when designing each of us.

We don't live long on this earth before we are stung by the sheer "unfairness" of such divinely ordered differentiation. At an early age we come to envy the superior strength, height, speed, or appearance of another boy. It takes longer, but the realization dawns soon enough that we are not as mentally astute, gregarious, witty, or charismatic as some of our peers.

In time such insights inform our self-assessment of pastoral capacity. First, I discern that God did not endow me with the most winning personality. Then I perceive that my personality limits the effectiveness of my ministry as an under-shepherd of God's flock. I don't want it to, but it does, and will continue to do so. For us duller types, this realization is a sting that keeps on stinging.

You naturally attain such insight by comparing yourself with more gifted pastors. This reality also slaps you in the face as members of your flock inform you by various ways and means that your personality does not compare favorably with other pastors they have known, or know about, or imagine they know about. They tell you in ways overt and covert that if only you had a more winsome personality the church would thrive or thrive more. Though hard to receive, you know such critique is not entirely devoid of truth. Hey, sometimes you even find yourself boring!

The good news unspectacular pastor is this: "winning personality" is not found in the list of pastoral qualifications in 1 Timothy chapter 3 or Titus chapter 1. What is writ large over those passages is character not charisma, faithfulness not magnetism, love for God's people not an alluring persona. Yes, you must earn the flock's trust. They must know that you are for them and steadfastly love them. It is not essential, however, that they find you charming, hilarious, dashing, or uniquely winsome. It's less important that they want to hang out with you. It's of utmost importance that they know you love God and that with warm zeal and welcoming invitation you long for them to follow Jesus with you all the way to glory (Col 1:28-29).

That said, how should we duller types respond to the debilitating effects of our prosaic constitutions? First, rejoice! Be happy, dull guy! God made you with sovereign purpose and fitted you with all the gifts necessary to fulfill any ministry he assigns to you. Might not a more charismatic man do a better job shepherding the flock you oversee? Only if the Chief Shepherd assigns that task to him. If Christ has commissioned you to shepherd a particular flock, rest in his sovereign purposes and faithfully lead that flock with all the love and skill God grants you. Refuse to cast envious eyes on the success of a more winsome shepherd. Weed jealousy from your soul. Stay focused on your standing in Christ.

Fulfill the stewardship he has entrusted to you.

Second, recognize that pastors with winning personalities face temptations we duller types seldom do. While unspectacular pastors tend to struggle with envy or self-pity, those with outsized personalities tend to struggle with prideful self-dependence and a dismissive spirit toward average souls. While they attract more enchanted followers, they also tend to leave more wounded sheep in their wake. Such observations are of scant consolation to those of us who would happily lug about the burden of a heavier backpack of charisma, yet there is grace to celebrate wherever we are spared temptation.

Third, refuse to settle. We duller types must not settle for pedestrian personalities. As you attend your heart, continue to analyze whether any aspect of your humdrum persona is rooted in laziness, selfishness, ingratitude, the fear of man, self-pity, a lack of love for others, or the like. If you are actively rooting out sin and progressing in Christlikeness, your persona will certainly improve. Don't settle. Keeping growing.

Fourth, learn to trust the power of Word and Spirit to accomplish what a winning personality never could. There are some freakishly gifted pastors out there whose personalities serve like a lamp to bugs on a summer night. But remember that while their winsomeness may attract more attention and open more doors of opportunity than you will ever experience, their gifting is incapable of effecting sanctification in the lives of Christ's flock. The church is formed and purified by Word and Spirit alone. So preach the Word persistently and faithfully. Depend upon the Spirit to save and sanctify souls, remembering McCheyne's maxim: "It is not great talents God blesses so much as great likeness to Jesus. A holy minister is an awful weapon in the hand of God" (R. M. McCheyne to Dan Edwards, Oct 2, 1840).

Ordinary pastors have a unique privilege to revel in the truth that "God chose what is weak in the world to shame the strong; God chose what is low and despised in the world ... so that no human being might boast in the presence of God" (1 Cor 1:27-29). We duller ones can uniquely revel in the truth that we hold the treasure of the gospel "in jars of clay" so as "to show that the surpassing power belongs to God and not to us" (2 Cor 4:7). That, ordinary pastor, is your glory: to see God work his surpassing power in and through your ministry despite your claypot-like weaknesses, or even because of them.

The Spirit uses ordinary means of grace to accomplish extraordinary works, and Christ uses ordinary stewards of that grace to broker extraordinary influence for his kingdom. Such lasting achievement is never effected by the power of one's personality. Ever. It is effected only by the power of the living God to save and transform souls. Before his eternal throne, and in his glorious presence, we will boast only of him. Forever.

ABOUT THE AUTHOR

Dan Miller is the senior pastor of Eden Baptist Church in Burnsville, Minnesota.

Are Buildings Essential to Building Healthy Churches?

Adam Sinnett

Are buildings necessary to building healthy churches? Does lacking a building put a church at a disadvantage? Does being mobile hinder disciple-making and the spread of the gospel?

THE DILEMMA EVERY PASTOR FACES

Every pastor I know whose church doesn't have a building wants one—and for good reason. Setting up and tearing down every Sunday is exciting, but only for a season. Recruiting faithful volunteers to arrive early and leave late—*every week*—is a challenge. Navigating relationships with landlords is often complex. Losing your space at the last minute is more common than you'd think. Finding a new space before the end of your current lease is time-consuming. This doesn't even include locating space for offices, classes, and mid-size gatherings throughout the week. This pastor is tempted to think, "If only we had a building…"

At the same time, almost every pastor I know whose church has a building, well, they want a slightly different one. After all, buildings can be too big or too small. The sanctuary may be just right, while there aren't enough classrooms. Or the kids' space may be ideal, but there aren't enough offices. Buildings are expensive to purchase, remodel, and maintain. Designated staff is typically required for facility management. The boiler always needs repair. (Why is it always the boiler?) Parking is usually a challenge, especially in urban contexts. This pastor is tempted to think, "If only our building had…"

PLACES AS STAGES

It's fascinating to survey the Scriptures and note the places where God tends to do redemptive work. Even a cursory reading reveals that God uses people in all kinds of places, from the everyday to the unexpected—from gardens, fields, arks, and prison cells to deserts, whale bellies, shipwrecks, and stables. But what's striking about this is that the places are always secondary. The places themselves are not the drama. They're merely the stages on which God's redemptive drama unfolds in ways big and small through the lives of his people.

So I wonder: why would we think it would be any different today? For those of us who may be tempted to think that God's work is somehow restricted or hindered by our space, we need this reminder.

THE PLACES OF DOWNTOWN CORNERSTONE

Our church gathers in the heart of downtown Seattle. We recently turned ten years old, and over the course of our shared life we've met in almost every conceivable type of space.

From birth to four, our Sunday gatherings took place in a basement-level antique shop, then an office building foyer, and then a movie theater (in fact, we met in five different theaters in the same complex over three years). We used conference rooms for classes. We offered pre-marital counseling in living rooms. We had prayer nights in a local community center. Our small groups met in condos, on rooftops, and throughout parks. Early morning discipleship groups met in cafes. Our staff worked out of a shoe-box sized office that had been donated to us.

And yet, Jesus used these scattered, everyday places as stages on which to spread the gospel, save sinners, and sanctify his people.

From year four to the present, we've leased a former dance club. This was incredibly significant for our fledgling church. It gave us a more permanent presence in our community. There was no more set-up and tear-down. We could consolidate all our ministry efforts to one central location.

But ... our sanctuary is too small, our office space is too limited, and we're kept from making any improvements by our landlords. Our family entrance is literally in an alley. We're glad to be in the most densely populated neighborhood downtown. But this area also attracts graffiti, urine, and drug deals. Oh, and did I mention it has no windows?

And yet Jesus is using this imperfect building as a stage on which to spread the gospel, save sinners, and sanctify his people.

From the beginning, we prayed, searched, and saved for a permanent building. We continually found ourselves coming up short. Some buildings were too small. Others were too expensive. Most were located outside the city center. Still others were purchased in cash by developers before the ink was dry on our own offer. But by God's grace, after ten years of searching and saving, we purchased a building in December 2020. While this is a huge piece of evidence of God's grace toward us, we now find ourselves leading a capital campaign and a building project. Meanwhile, amid a once-in-a-century pandemic, the cost of raw materials has soared.

Buildings are a gift, but they too have their challenges.

THE ADVANTAGES/ DISADVANTAGES OF NOT HAVING A BUILDING

Her are a few *advantages* of being mobile:

- Your church isn't tied down to a particular place.
- There's no financial burden of a mortgage.
- As your church grows, you can simply move to a larger space.

- Generally, your landlord is responsible for facility repairs.

But there are, of course, some *disadvantages*:

- Your experience will often be determined by your landlord.
- Set up and tear down requires significant energy and volunteer capital.
- You will often be thinking about where to meet next.
- Lacking a permanent space can communicate a lack of rootedness to the community.

THE ADVANTAGES/ DISADVANTAGES OF HAVING A BUILDING

Here are a few *advantages* of owning a building:

- A permanent building communicates stability and presence.
- You no longer need to set up and tear down every week.
- You no longer need to be concerned with lease negotiations, landlords, or finding new spaces.
- Your church is usually easier to find.
- You have more freedom to make facility improvements.

But there are some *disadvantages*, too:

- Buildings can be expensive and require ongoing repair.
- They often need staff attention.
- If the building is too small, you'll need to find another space or invest in an expensive renovation.
- If the building is too big, your church may have difficulty supporting it.
- If it's in a poor location, it may not serve the church well.

CONCLUSION

So, are buildings essential to building healthy churches? No. Can they be incredibly helpful? Absolutely.

Is God's work limited by your space? No. Does having a building guarantee more fruitfulness? No. Does a building make all your physical space issues go away? No.

Now here's the trickiest question: should a church get a building if it can? In most cases, I'd say yes.

The benefits outweigh the burdens. Above all, whether we have a building or not, we need to remember that our space is merely one stage on which God's redemptive drama continues to unfold.

ABOUT THE AUTHOR

Adam Sinnett is the Lead pastor of Downtown Cornerstone Church in Seattle, Washington.

Congregational Singing: Can Musical Style Dilute This Ordinary Means of Grace?

Neal Woollard

As a somewhat creatively minded musician, writing with clarity has always been a challenge. I have a point in my mind, and it feels clear and compelling—until I write it down. The words I use to make my point sometimes dilute the point. I try to do too much. I think I'm doing something cool like making a play on words, but instead I'm muddying the water. I have to work hard on my writing style to clarify my points, not dilute my points.

The same can be said for musical style in church worship music. Does the style clarify or dilute the main point, i.e., congregational singing? A singing church is a means of grace as a Spirit-dwelt congregation gathered by grace exhorts one towards faithfulness as they worship God. The entire church speaks the rich Word of Christ to one another.

So here's the question: does your musical style make it clear that this is the main event? Or does the singing of the church get lost because the style is trying to do too much?

I want to make a simple case: the more clearly our worship style puts the focus on the congregation singing, the less we dilute this means of grace. To work this idea out, we'll look at congregational singing as a means of grace. I'll then define what I mean by worship style, and close by applying what we've learned.

A COMPELLING MEANS OF GRACE

Congregational singing is the sound of a people saved by grace. After God saves his people by grace, they sing (Exod. 15; Acts 2; Rev. 15). Delivered from the world, they no longer belong to or look like the world.

In the New Covenant, what's one way the Spirit leads us to godliness? By the church singing (Eph. 5:18-19). How do we know the rich Word of Christ dwells in us? By the church singing (Col. 3:16). The Word of Christ reverberates as the Spirit-indwelt people of Christ exhort and encourage one another.

And what a compelling means of grace this is! A singing church is hard to ignore. It's audible and visual. It's tangible and mystical. It's individual and corporate. It's cognitive and emotional.

If the Spirit wants to grow us in grace by the sound of the church singing, then that's where we should put all the focus. As the music leader at our church, I want people walking away from our gatherings having heard the Word of God in the mouths of the people of God. How do we try to do this? That brings us to the question of style.

STYLE – DOES IT CLARIFY OR DILUTE?

Style can clarify or dilute congregational singing. If congregational singing is what we are doing, style is how we do it. It's the form church music takes through things like genre, instrumentation, and the use of lighting and sound. We must remember: there's freedom and joy in different styles! After all, a particular style isn't prescribed, but a particular goal is—congregational singing.

So we must ask a few follow-up questions: does our style clearly present congregational singing as the main event? Or does it muddy the water? Can we hear our church? Are the melodies singable? Like a preacher honing his craft to clearly present the Word of God, we want to hone our craft to present the Word of God through singing. The sneaky thing about style is that it can become the end in of itself. When style becomes the what instead of the how, the richness of congregational singing is diluted.

I'm still learning how to do this better. I've been playing in worship teams since I was twelve. I've led singing for over twenty years. I'm grateful for the variety of experiences I've had—from small churches to large churches, from campfires to skate parks to jam-packed stadiums, from bright stages with big sound to little amplification and no extra light, from classical hymns to modern songs. Every step of the way, I sincerely wanted to see God's people worship him with full hearts and voices. But those experiences and God's patient instruction have convinced me that style is more important than we realize.

I could make many applications about this, but I'll focus on three—genre, sound and lighting, and creativity.

GENRE

While our churches are diverse, our church music often isn't. We should delight in singing diverse kinds of music because God is saving a diverse people! In other words, don't just sing new songs. Or just sing old songs. Or songs just from your ethnic heritage. Or just songs you like as a music leader. Sing rich theological songs you may not even like because you know someone else will like it. Sing songs that built up the church in ages past.

This shifts our focus beyond individual expression and compels us to sing in a way that glorifies God and encourages other members. We're forced to notice how God's Word is dwelling richly in those in my church and how God's Word has dwelt richly in churches throughout the world, which should makes us want to exalt Christ more!

In short, our style should honor the diversity of the people God has saved and continues to save.

SOUND AND LIGHTING

What does our sound and lighting tell the church member they should experience? In the past, I used the phrase "a worship experience" to talk about church gatherings. I've since realized that this phrase isn't helpful because it can accidentally communicate that the goal in corporate worship is some kind of subjective, emotional experience. That's not the case.

However, it's still true that our singing should cover the full range of human experience. Consider Israel's hymnbook, the Psalms.

It should be obvious that sound and lighting can either dilute or clarify that our goal in corporate worship is congregational singing. We should do everything we can to make that the primary experience—not whatever's happening on stage. It's reductionistic to say that congregational singing can't happen when the lights are dark above the congregation and the sound on stage is loud.

But we should be honest about how we're using these tools—are they highlighting the experience of a few or the whole congregation? We should turn down the sound enough so that the congregation is the primary engine. We should push up the dimmer faders so that we can actually see the congregation and, as a result, concentrate our experience on the whole church speaking to one another in psalms, hymns, and spiritual songs.

CREATIVITY

With all this focus on the congregation, am I implying that musical creativity and musical beauty isn't important? Not at all! I'd argue that it takes creativity to play music that clarifies and doesn't dilute congregational singing. Creativity informs style. So like style, creativity is not something we do, but how we do something. In particular, I would argue for a pastorally sensitive, biblically informed creativity.

Who doesn't want to be known as a church with good music? But Spirit-animated and

Spirit-directed creativity asks more than "How'd the music sound?" It asks, "Did everything we do serve the singing of our whole church?" This doesn't diminish creativity; it aims it toward a goal.

Creativity matures beyond self-expression to humble service to all. This shift should be evident. Here are a few examples:

Creativity prizes musical simplicity that doesn't overpower the voice of the church; it adorns the voice of the church, pushing it forward.

Creativity shapes our instincts so that we know when to highlight joy and when to move toward lament.

Creativity uses fills that aren't just cool riffs, but function as cues for the congregation to sing.

Creativity teaches the band to find joy in cutting out often so that the church can hear itself sing.

Creativity teaches even sound engineers to mix so that the congregation is the main instrument.

CONCLUSION

Last Sunday I was leading the singing and I was tired. It had been a heavy week and the weight of the week hung over me. But that heaviness quickly evaporated as I heard our church sing "How Firm a Foundation" and "Christ Is Mine Forevermore." As their words washed over me, I remembered God's steadfast, unshakable love for his people. I needed to be encouraged to grow in the grace of Jesus. And you know what? That's precisely what happened ... as my entire church sang psalms, hymns, and spiritual songs over me.

What a kind means of grace. Let's do everything we can to let our style bring clarity to this means of grace, not dilute it.

ABOUT THE AUTHOR

Neal Woollard is the Worship & Discipleship Director at Hinson Baptist Church in Portland, Oregon.

Yes, Scripture Reading Really Does Change People

Terry Johnson

I grew up in a typical evangelical church of the 1960s and 70s. Specifically, it was the First Baptist Church of Dominguez, a Missionary Baptist Church nestled between Carson and Long Beach, California. It was a Bible-believing, gospel-preaching, altar-call-featuring church connected denominationally with a number of churches in Southern California and the farm-rich California central valleys. These congregations initially consisted of families that fled the Dust Bowl and the hardships of the Depression to start anew in the West. Ours was a good church, an evangelical church, a faithful church, as were its sister churches.

And yet, I don't recall ever hearing the Scripture read during a church service aside from the few verses upon which the sermon was based.

EVANGELICAL NEGLECT

What was true of my neighborhood church was true of all of Southern California's large evangelical churches that I visited at one time or another during my teens and early 20s: Swindoll's Evangelical Free Church of Fullerton, Chuck Smith's Calvary Chapel, Ray Ortlund's Lake Avenue Congregational, David Hocking's Grace Brethren of Long Beach, MacArthur's Grace Community Church, and Lloyd John Ogilvie's 1st Presbyterian Church of Hollywood. Substantial Bible reading simply wasn't a feature of evangelical churches of that time and that place. Neither, I suspect, has it become a feature of typical evangelical churches today.

ANGLICAN CONTRAST

I spent two years attending an Anglican theological college, Trinity, in Bristol, England. This meant attending a plethora of local Anglican churches: low church, high church, liberal, and conservative. They all held one thing in common: the *Prayer Book* and the substantial Bible reading as mandated by the lectionary. These readings ran the gamut: Old Testament, New Testament epistles, Gospels, psalms.

The irony was rich and continues to be.

By and large, evangelicals in the United States do not read the Bible in their public services. Anglicans, some of whom are liberal skeptics, few of whom believe in inerrancy, do. Strange.

Why don't evangelical churches read the Bible? I could come to only one conclusion: *they don't think it's important.* Considerable time in their services is given to singing and preaching and announcements and perhaps even to informal chatter. Yet Scripture reading is omitted, apart from the verses to be preached. Why? I repeat: They don't seem to think it's that important. They don't see value in it. It might be or is likely to be boring. And so, Bible-believing, inerrancy-defending evangelical churches don't perceive enough value in simple Bible reading to give it a place in their public services.

SCRIPTURE'S SELF-TESTIMONY

In *Worshipping with Calvin*, I give examples of people transformed by the simple public reading of Scripture, including one J. C. Ryle (1816–1900).

However, evangelicals shouldn't require anecdotal testimonies of the transformative power of Scripture reading. After all, we have Scripture's own self-testimony. Are we not said to be born again by the "living and abiding word"? Do we not come to faith by "*hearing* the word of Christ"? Do we not grow by the pure milk of God's Word? Are we not sanctified by the truth of God's Word? Is the Word of grace not able to build us up and give us an eternal inheritance? Is the gospel Word of truth not constantly bearing fruit and increasing? Is the Word of God not living and active and sharper than a two-edged sword? Is the gospel not the power of God for salvation? I could go on (1 Peter 1:23–25; Rom 10:17; 1 Peter 2:2; Jn 17:17; Acts 20:32; Col 1:6; Heb 4:12; Rom 1:16; cf Eph 6:1; 1 Thess 2:13; 2 Tim 3:15; Jer 23:29; Is 55:11; 1 Thess 1:5; Jas 1:21).

MY TURNING POINT

The turning point for me came on a stormy autumn night in 1977. Several Trinity students and I walked across the Bristol Downs to St. Mary's Redcliff Parrish church, a conservative Anglican congregation. Around mid-service, a man stood to present the Old Testament reading from the prophet Isaiah. He read slowly, carefully, and with emphasis. The effect was powerful. No, it was dynamic.

Then the irony hit me. I began to ask, "Why do we evangelicals not include extended *lectio continua* reading of Scripture (the historic Reformed practice) in our churches?" Of course Scripture reading can be boring. But *any* element of worship can be poorly administered. That's why we should take care to read Scripture skillfully. The reader should be well-acquainted with the text so as to read with understanding and nuance. Let's face it. The fear of boring a congregation is a lame excuse.

CONCLUSION

If we believe Scripture's self-testimony, we cannot perpetuate the neglect of substantial, systematic Bible reading in the public services of the church. It is one of only five items identified in the *Westminster*

Confession of Faith (XXI.3-5) and its sister confessions (London, Savoy) as necessary elements of a worship service regulated by God's Word. The Westminster Assembly's sister document, the Directory for the Public Worship of God, recommends a chapter from each testament in each of the two Sunday services.

At least a chapter would be a good place to start.

ABOUT THE AUTHOR

Terry Johnson is the senior minster of Independent Presbyterian Church in Savannah, Georgia.

Yes, The Ordinances Really Do Change People

Tiago Oliveira

Evangelicals are the descendants of the Protestant Reformation. We believe that salvation is by grace alone, through faith alone, in Christ alone. Among other things, the Reformers rejected the Catholic Church's sacramental system, which misconstrued baptism and the Lord's Supper as instrumental for salvation.

However, just because Protestants rejected the ordinances as instrumental for salvation doesn't mean they're not necessary in the Christian life. We believe the Lord Jesus instituted the ordinances for the people of God to observe when they gather for worship. They're a sign of the Christian's union both with Christ and with one another.

And so, we believe the ordinances really do change people. Let me give you three reasons why.

1. THE ORDINANCES ARE THE WORD MADE VISIBLE.

The ordinances are inherently tied to the Word of God. Furthermore, it's by the Word of God that unbelievers come to faith (Rom 10:13–17) and Christians become like Jesus (John 17:17). As the church gathers for worship, the Word stands at the center of our gatherings—through our praying and preaching, our reading and our singing, and through our practice of baptism and the Lord's Supper. These ordinances are the Word made visible.

Our Lord Jesus instituted both baptism (Matt 28:18–20) and the Lord's Supper (Luke 22:14–20; 1 Cor. 11:23-30). They are part of God's plans for the edification of his church. He commands his church to observe baptism and the Lord's supper because they are profitable for us as a means for our sanctification. Just as with the Word of God, the ordinances are not magical in themselves. But yes! They really do change people.

2. THE ORDINANCES POINT TO OUR UNION WITH CHRIST—AND OUR UNION WITH ONE ANOTHER.

The ordinances are visible signs of the gospel. What does that mean? Let me explain.

In baptism, we see the gospel represented in the immersion of the repentant sinner. Through baptism, their sin has been "washed away" (Acts 22:16); their baptism proclaims that they are united to Christ in his death and resurrection (Col. 2:11–12; cf. Rom. 6:3–4).

In the Lord's Supper, we see the gospel portrayed when a local church, as one body, partakes of the Bread and the Cup (1 Cor. 10:16–17). The Lord's Supper is a memorial meal in which the body of Christ remembers Christ's body which he gave in the place of his people and Christ's blood which he shed to establish the new covenant.

These symbols are not abstract. They visibly display invisible truths—of salvation, regeneration, and union with Christ. That's why Christ gave these symbols to the church. Those who participate in the ordinances ought to be Christians, such that the visible representation matches the invisible reality. In other words, yes, the ordinances change people. But they also point to *changed* people. Here's what I mean.

When we got baptized, we identified with both our repentance (Acts 2:38; cf. Rom 6:3–4) and our regeneration, that is, our new life in Christ (John 3:5–7; Rom. 6:4). Furthermore, we publicly affirmed our commitment not only to God, but also to his people. This latter commitment is crystallized through the Lord's Supper, in which the local church comes together to remember the death of the Lord Jesus and anticipate the day when he will return (1 Cor. 11:23–26).

If we read through 1 Corinthians 11, it's clear that a proper participation in the Lord's Supper requires self-examination (1 Cor. 11:28). It requires asking at least two questions: How's our relationship with the Lord? And how's our relationship with fellow believers?

The Lord's Supper invites us to remember Christ's work on our behalf, and to recommit our lives to God. This kind of self-examination leads to repentance. Change is an inherent part of the ordinances. In other words, yes, the ordinances really do change people.

3. THE ORDINANCES REALLY MEAN SOMETHING.

Finally, the way Scripture talks about the ordinances should convince us that they really change people. In his first letter, Peter says that "baptism … now saves you, not as a removal of dirt from the body but as an appeal to God for a good conscience, through the resurrection of Jesus Christ" (1 Pet. 3:21; cf. Rom. 6:3–4; Col. 2:11-12). Note that it is not the water that saves but the appeal to God through the resurrection of Jesus Christ. Still, it's significant that baptism can be said to "save." How do we make sense of this, given what I said earlier about baptism *not* being necessary for salvation?

We might compare it to a couple getting married. The man and the woman could just get together and have a private, mutual agreement. But a public ceremony with a public oath before witnesses—that's a visible contract, and it changes everything. In the wedding ceremony, the man and the woman, upon their public oath, are declared to be husband and wife. In the same way, in baptism, the person—upon their public profession of faith—is recognized by the church to be a Christian. The baptized person now enters into a new life, a new identity, a new allegiance. They belong to a new people.

Concerning the Lord's Supper, Paul asks the Corinthians: "The cup of blessing that we bless, is it not a participation in the blood of Christ? The bread that we break, is it not a participation in the body of Christ? Because there is one bread, we who are many are one body, for we all partake of the one bread" (1 Cor. 10:16–17; cf. John 6:53–58).

The cup and the bread are visible, material signs. But when the members of a local church partake of these elements, they become something more. They become the means by which we fellowship with Christ and one another. That's why Paul later says that "you cannot partake in the table of the Lord and the table of demons" (1 Cor. 10:21). When we're participating rightly, there's true communion with God and with one another. When we're *not* participating rightly, we're communing with something else.

Of course, the baptismal water, the loaf of bread, and the cup do not have in them magical properties. Just as the words of Scripture need to be believed to be profitable to us, so also the ordinances need to be received in faith in order to be profitable to us. In other words, yes, the ordinances really do change people. But faith must come first.

ABOUT THE AUTHOR

Tiago Oliveira is a member of Capitol Hill Baptist Church and a PhD student (Biblical Studies) at Puritan Reformed Theological Seminary.

Yes, Preaching Really Does Change People

Mike Bullmore

If you've been in pastoral ministry for any length of time at all you've asked the question: Is my preaching actually *doing* anything? Is it having any effect?

The question could be addressed on several different grounds. It could be addressed on historical grounds, pointing to the powerful effects of preaching in various times and places in the history of the church, notably, from the beginning in the book of Acts. It could be addressed on personal grounds by means of collected anecdotes—"Let me tell you about Joe and Mary Black and what God did in their lives through the faithful preaching of God's Word."

But without question, the most compelling response is going to be a theological one, grounded in the realities presented in Scripture regarding who God is, what he is doing, what his Word does, and what he fully intends preaching to accomplish.

AN UNDER-CELEBRATED CHARACTERISTIC

We rightly celebrate the authority, the trustworthiness, and the sufficiency of Scripture. But perhaps an under-celebrated characteristic of Scripture is its efficacy. By "efficacy" I simply mean the ability to actually accomplish what is intended.

Probably the clearest statement on the efficacy of Scripture is found in Isaiah 55:10–11:

> For as the rain and the snow come down from heaven and do not return there but water the earth, making it bring forth and sprout, giving seed to the sower and bread to the eater, so shall my word be that goes out from my mouth; it shall not return to me empty, *but it shall accomplish that which I purpose, and shall succeed in the thing for which I sent it.* (italics added)

That's a powerful statement on the efficacy of God's Word, and it provides more than sufficient grounds for a deep conviction in the heart of every faithful preacher. Without this conviction, a pastor will regularly wonder about and doubt the usefulness of his preaching. But with this conviction fully in place a pastor will have every reason to persevere in his regular and faithful exposition of God's Word.

WHAT GOD'S WORD IS & DOES

Think of the images the Bible uses to speak of God's Word. It's like a sword (Hebrews 4:12). It's like a hammer (Jeremiah 23:29). These images evoke powerful efficacy. Even the less aggressive images of rain (Isaiah 55:10) and seed (Mark 4:14) speak of efficacy.

And think of all the things the Bible says God's Word can do.

- It brings about faith. "Faith comes from hearing, and hearing through the word of Christ" (Romans 10:17).
- It gives new spiritual life. "You have been born again, not of perishable seed but of imperishable, the living and abiding word of God" (1 Peter 1:23).
- It helps us grow. "Like newborn infants, long for the pure spiritual milk, that by it you may grow up to salvation" (1 Peter 2:2).
- It sanctifies us. "Sanctify them in the truth; your word is truth" (John 17:17).
- It searches and convicts. "For the word of God is living and active, sharper than any two-edged sword, piercing to the

division of soul and of spirit, of joints and of marrow, and discerning the thoughts and intentions of the heart" (Hebrews 4:12).
- It liberates. "If you abide in my word, you are truly my disciples, and you will know the truth, and the truth will set you free" (John 8:31–32).
- It refreshes and renews. "Give me life according to your word" (Psalm 119:25).
- It revives our souls and rejoices our hearts. "The law of the Lord is perfect, reviving the soul … the precepts of the Lord are right, rejoicing the heart" (Psalm 19:7,8).

These are all things the Bible claims God's Word can do in our lives! And there's so much more! So is it any wonder that David says, "Blessed is the man who walks not in the counsel of the wicked, nor stands in the way of sinners, nor sits in the seat of scoffers; but his delight is in the law of the LORD, and on his law he meditates day and night. He is like a tree …" (Psalm 1:1–3)? And the amazing thing is that God has ordained preaching as the primary means by which this powerful Word is brought effectively to human beings (cf. 2 Timothy 4:2).

WHAT'S AT STAKE

There's so much at stake in our preaching. People's lives are at stake. People are lost, alienated from God, and desperately in need of hearing the saving Word of Christ. The health of Christ's church is at stake. God's people desperately need instruction and encouragement from God's Word. When God said to Ezekiel, "Can these bones live?" it didn't look very promising. But God instructed him to preach and the result was absolutely marvelous. (Read the wonderful account of this in Ezekiel 37:1–14. Pay special attention to the very last line.)

There are some particularly emboldening words found in the early chapters of Deuteronomy. Very significantly, these words are often repeated by Jesus himself: "Man does not live by bread alone, but man lives by every word that comes from the mouth of the LORD" (Deuteronomy 8:3;

Matthew 4:4). Don't miss that. Man lives by God's Word!

This is why God has called us to preach. Natural, unregenerate man comes to life by the Word of God. And having been brought to life by the Word, the regenerate man continues to be sustained and nourished by God's Word. Peter said it so well. In a moment of spirit-inspired brilliance he spoke this truth, "Where else would we go, you have the words of life" (John 6:68).

Fellow preacher, God has promised that through this apparently weak and frail means, using weak and frail creatures like us, he will accomplish much. He has said so. He has promised to do it. Believe what God has said. The faithful preaching of God's Word accomplishes much.

So, steady on brother. Do your work and then let the Word do its work, a work almighty God has promised will be done.

ABOUT THE AUTHOR

Mike Bullmore is senior pastor at CrossWay Community Church in Bristol, Wisconsin, and a Council member of The Gospel Coalition. He is a contributor to the ESV Men's Devotional Bible.

Yes, Singing Really Does Change People

Shai Linne

When I was converted to Christianity as an adult over twenty years ago, I vividly recall my first Sunday at my mother's church. At the time, I had very little frame of reference for what a church service might look like. Growing up, I only stepped into a church building for the occasional funeral. My mother and a few of the Christians I knew had invited me to church for years—a request I would always politely decline as I scoffed inwardly at the very thought that I could possibly need salvation.

But now, everything was different. Weeks earlier I had given my life to Christ after reading the Gospel of John. Suddenly, I saw the world through new eyes. Though I didn't know anything about church, my thought was that if there was a group of people who were as eager as I was to celebrate my precious Lord Jesus who had so powerfully revealed Himself to me, I was all for it!

As I entered the building, I was immediately struck by the festive, welcoming atmosphere. As I walked to my seat, nameless saints stopped me numerous times to greet me with a warm hug. Some told me they had been praying for me for years. Once the music began, everyone stood and completely gave themselves to "praise and worship" for the next hour. There was singing, clapping, dancing, and shouting. The full-bodied engagement of the congregation clearly indicated that God is a big deal and that it was important to make much of him.

Every song was completely new to me. But as soon as I learned the melodies, I joined right in. One song in particular captured the joy and simplicity of my newfound love for God and the gospel:

Lord, I lift your name on high
Lord, I love to sing your praises
I'm so glad you're in my life
I'm so glad you came to save us

You came from heaven to earth
To show the way
From the earth to the cross
My debt to pay
From the cross to the grave
From the grave to the sky
Lord, I lift your name on high

In those early years of my walk with the Lord, I viewed singing in the church primarily as a means of worshiping God by reflecting on my salvation, like in the song above. What I hadn't considered as much is the idea of singing as a means of grace for the sanctification of believers.

When you think about sanctification, what comes to mind? Most of us would mention things like Scripture, faith, the Holy Spirit, trials, temptation, suffering, and prayer. All of those certainly play a role in making us more like Jesus. But over the years, I've come to appreciate the role that singing plays in helping both individual believers and congregations to grow in the grace and knowledge of the Lord Jesus Christ.

In 2 Corinthians 3, the Apostle Paul contrasts the glory of the law of Moses with the greater glory of the New Covenant revealed in the person and work of Jesus Christ. In verse 18, he gives a powerful description of how followers of Christ are sanctified: "And we all, with unveiled face, beholding the glory of the Lord, are being transformed into the same image from one degree of glory to another" (2 Cor. 3:18).

A few verses later, we see that this glorious sanctifying work is empowered by God's Word as the Apostles openly state the truth found in the Scriptures. We usually associate this with sermons or Bible studies or private devotions—and rightly so. But have you considered that this transformation can also occur as we sing to one another in psalms and hymns and spiritual songs (Eph. 5:19)? Yes, singing really changes people!

We certainly see this in the numerous psalms that find the psalmist dealing with distress, difficulty, doubt, or discouragement and ultimately conclude with expressions of renewed trust and hope in God (see Psalms 3, 22, 31:9–24, 38, 73, among others). What the psalmists experienced wasn't merely a better mood, but something profoundly spiritual: increased faith in and love for God, qualities that can only be produced by the Holy Spirit. The Psalms were the original hymnbook of God's people. As the church has echoed these psalms throughout the ages, countless believers have experienced the same kinds of spiritual changes that the original writers did when they first penned them.

This also applies in our day as we sing songs that are saturated with Scripture and the gospel. God's Word does not return to him void, whether it's preached or sung. The gospel is the power of God for the salvation of all who believe, whether it's read silently or vocalized melodically. There are few things in this world more powerful than a gathering of Christians joyfully and passionately singing God's praises together, submitting themselves to the truth of God's Word and reminding themselves that they are united around Jesus Christ crucified, risen, and exalted.

How often has your faith in Christ been strengthened, your appreciation for the gospel deepened, the allure of sin weakened, and your love for God heightened—all as you sang Scripture-infused, gospel-centered songs with the gathered assembly?

This isn't accidental. This is 2 Corinthians 3:18 at work. This is the kindness of our heavenly Father who loves to give good gifts to his people for our joy and his glory.

I'm convinced that there is far more happening in our church services than most of us are actually aware of. Hebrews 6 hints at this when it speaks of our participating in the "powers of the age to come." I don't know the fullness of what this means, but the sanctifying power of the Holy Spirit is surely included. Of course, we'll easily miss it if we're distracted by the argument we had before church, the loudness of the keyboard during church, or our lunch plans after church. But if we entered the corporate gathering with an expectation that God would actually change us, we might find ourselves weeping with gratitude as we sing about sinners losing all their guilty stains. We might be moved to repentance when we confess yet again in song that we're prone to wander and leave the God we love. We might be overcome with awe as we address the holy, holy, holy, merciful and mighty, God in three persons, blessed trinity. We might have increased confidence to face Monday because on Sunday, we were reminded that as he stands in victory, sin's curse has lost its grip on me.

One of the traditions at our church is to sing the benediction to one another at the end of our gatherings. Adapted from 2 Corinthians 13:13, we sing:

May the grace of our Lord Jesus Christ
And the love of God the Father
And the Holy Spirit's presence abide
With you now, and with you forever
With you now, and with you forever

As we sing, we look around at our brothers and sisters and literally encourage one another with Scripture set to music. And each week, my story is the same. No matter what I may have felt coming into church or how challenging the previous week may have been, those moments of eye contact with the saints as we participate in that holy serenade do something—not just *for* me, but *in* me. I can't always pinpoint it, but by faith I know that after we sing, I'm not quite the same as I was when I walked in. It's not always earth-shattering, but there's a difference and it's supernatural.

In other words, singing really does change people.

ABOUT THE AUTHOR

Shai Linne is a Christian hip-hop artist and author. Shai is a member at Risen Christ Fellowship in Philadelphia, PA.

How I Accidentally Stumbled Across-And Then Fell in Love with-the Ordinary Means of Grace

Alex Duke

I want to tell you about the most influential sermon I've ever heard.

I. THE TRANSATLANTIC DRIVE, PART 1

I went to college a year later than most of my friends, so by the time I showed up they had already been going to a church for a year. I won't say its name, but it had the word "Baptist" in it. I, on the other hand, liked to attend churches whose names could have doubled as tech start-ups or rehab centers: The Verve, The Well, Crossroads, you know what I'm talking about.

But I trusted my friends. So I sleepily got in the car on Sunday morning and drove 15 miles *away* from campus to a cross-topped building nestled between two fields. The cattle were lowing, indeed. For a collegiate underclassman, this 20-minute jaunt felt like a transatlantic journey. I wondered if I'd ever return to it.

II. THE PLAIN PREACHER

We walked inside, I sat down, we sang some songs, I sat down again, and then this older man stood up in front of us. He wore a suit, forgettably dark and non-tailored. I noticed immediately that there was no podium, no pulpit, no music stand—just a stool which I expected him to sit on in order to look casual and conversational. I'd seen pastors do that before. He didn't strike me as the conversational type. As it turns out, the stool was more for his Bible, which was big and heavy and well-worn. It looked like it had been through the same things this man had been through.

I don't know how else to put it other than to say that this man looked aggressively *ordinary*. He could have passed for my pharmacist, or your son's Little League coach, or a guy who sells bait at a tackle shop.

And then he started preaching. "Open your Bibles to Genesis 6:1–8." He spoke slowly, with a carefulness that to some could be mistaken as uncertainty.

What happened over the next 40 minutes was as bewildering as it was beautiful. Now, I'd grown up in church. I'd read Christian books and led Christian Bible studies. I could explain how trusting in Jesus changes everything, and I could have probably articulated the teleological argument for the existence of God. I'd raised my hands in worship; I'd wept at my own sins and the sins of my friends.

I *loved* Jesus.

But I'd never heard anything like this. Because this plain-looking preacher with his well-worn Bible and his kind-of-pointless stool just stood there, explaining and applying Genesis 6 to all who would listen. And *I* listened, transfixed.

The sermon wasn't polished—years later he told me he just can't use a manuscript, though he wishes he could—but it was precise. It was sharp and sincere. He called us "dear ones." He was meek—so, so, so meek. And yet, when he spoke of the judgment of God on sinners like us, his meekness yielded to a firm urgency. He told us to flee to the ark that is Christ. He told us not to mock at the coming judgment of God, and he pled with us to revel in the mercy of Christ before the waters of judgment rose above our necks.

From Genesis 6, he talked to us, with tears in his eyes—he always ended up having tears in his eyes—about God's love for sinners like us. He talked to us about Jesus and substitution and resurrection.

III. DR. WATSON!

I'm not sure he taught me any discrete fact I didn't already know. Instead, like a good detective, he laid out everything I already knew in such a way that it led to a conclusion. But here's what floored me: his conclusion wasn't about *me* or about *what I should do*. It was a conclusion about Christ, a conclusion about how God had given us the sixth chapter of Genesis not primarily to teach us about the righteousness of Noah, but the righteousness of Christ.

If you'd asked me, during my first transatlantic journey to church, to read Genesis 6 and explain to you what it meant, I have no idea what I would have said. You could have given me Sherlock Holmes' own personal magnifying glass and I'm not sure I would have found a single clue that led to the cross. Of course, I knew from experiences that sermons *had to end* at the cross, but I thought the Lord allowed teleportation, especially for sermons that focused on the Old Testament.

That's the story of the first expositional sermon I ever heard. I loved it. It stimulated me intellectually *and* spiritually. But I had no category for it. I had no idea what was happening, and I had even less of an idea *why* it was happening. To be honest, I found it as curious and idiosyncratic as I found it compelling.

Perhaps the preacher just had a really good week, I thought. *I wonder what he'll do the next week.*

IV. THE TRANSATLANTIC DRIVE, PART 2

And so, next Sunday, I sleepily got back in the car again—walked inside, sat down, sang some songs, sat down, and then the preacher stood up. He wore a different suit but held the same Bible.

He began with the same slow, sleepy intro: "Open your Bibles to Genesis 6. We'll begin in Verse 9."

I tapped my friend on the shoulder and whispered, "This is weird.

What's he doing?" He laughed. I didn't. I was lost. I'd never seen a preacher just pick up where he left off, like an episode of *24* or something.

For the next 40 minutes, the preacher preached from the book of Genesis yet again. The shape of the sermon was the same, but its contours had changed according to the passage in question. And so I listened again, transfixed again.

At this point, I realized what I'd heard the week before wasn't just a one-off. It was a way to *do church*, a way to think about the Christian life. I couldn't believe I'd never heard of it before, and I couldn't wait to learn more.

That's why this second expositional sermon was the most influential sermon I ever heard. It sparked in me a shocking revelation: I've been missing out on something I never knew existed.

V. A BUSTED DAM

Nearly four years later, on one of my last Sundays in college, I heard a sermon about Joseph's bones. The preacher—by now I called him "Pastor Steve"—pointed to the resurrection of God's people on the last day and pled with us to trust in Jesus. Our text that morning? Genesis 50:22–26. Of course he called us "dear ones." And of course there were tears in his eyes.

There were tears in my eyes, too.

I loved this man, my pastor and my preacher. He was ordinary, he wore dark suits in the dog days of summer, and he cried literally every single Sunday. But that's not why I loved him. I loved him because he introduced me to God's extraordinary grace in such an ordinary way—through simple, Word-centered sermons that didn't rely on relatable stories or conclude with a clarion call to moral renovation. His sermons were *to* me, of course, but they weren't *about* me. They were about God and the gospel.

Though I didn't realize it, I showed up to this church with a dammed-up head—full of true information about the Bible and sincere feelings on how to live a life that pleases Jesus. But I didn't really know what to do with all this, and I certainly couldn't make sense of the Bible. I didn't know how to understand it and apply it and connect it all to Jesus. I knew so many discrete facts, and I felt so many discrete convictions. But no one had showed me how they *fit*.

Over time, Pastor Steve's sermons connected the dots. They were the hands that thrust the sword of the Spirit into my mind and heart. They pierced the dam, and, in the process, this ordinary man and his ordinary sermons brought extraordinary change to my ordinary life.

On my first Sunday there, I showed up at that church wondering if I'd ever return to it. The drive was so long, and the vibe was so *meh*. On my last Sunday there, I left wondering if I would ever find a church just like it.

ABOUT THE AUTHOR

Alex Duke is the editorial manager of 9Marks. He lives in Louisville, Kentucky, where he also works at Third Avenue Baptist Church as the Director of Youth Ministry and Ecclesiological Training.

Never Underestimate the Value of Ordinary, Brief, Christian Conversations

Caleb Greggsen

Language learning is a time-intensive activity, and language students sometimes dread those long hours of concentrated study, when their head is down in a book or they're sitting in a language class. They forget they're also learning the language when, in a foreign nation, they listen to the radio, watch cartoons with their kids, or enjoy conversations with the old men at the post office. None of those are intensely focused opportunities, but they count as exposure nonetheless, and a language student can be intentional with them.

IN PRAISE OF CHRISTIAN CONVERSATIONS

Most Christians—and dare I say, pastors—fall into a similar error when it comes to Christian discipleship. We count the big stuff. The things we can put in our calendar. And because we neglect to notice the myriad small discipling moments, we neglect to utilize them. We overlook the value of ordinary, brief, Christian conversations.

Pastor, consider how many brief interactions do you normally have in those 20 to 30 minutes at the back door after your sermon? What questions do you hear? What situations do you learn about? Who do you get to care for, just a few minutes before they walk into their week?

In such moments, I learn a marriage is in trouble. I counsel a brother whose boss pressured him to lie to a client. I apologize to a member I offended by some careless word. I usually meet many non-Christians there. It's a vital time.

Now multiply my handful of interactions throughout the rest of our members. How many conversations happen in that room? And you know what? In every single interaction, there's an opportunity for Christians to influence one another, for the gospel to be conveyed and clarified and applied. These opportunities aren't typically impressive or even memorable—but they're cumulatively significant.

Now, I'm certainly not claiming that these conversations are *always* deeply spiritual. That's not the case in my congregation, and it's probably not the case in yours. Odds are, many of them are about the game last night, or the game that's about to start, or just a repeat of the same conversation that happened last week and will happen against next week: "How are you?" "Busy. You?" "Same."

TWO ASSERTIONS

I want to make two assertions about these conversations: they're more significant than we think, and they can become even more significant than we think.

A passing comment can have an enduring influence on someone's life. How many times have you had a member bring up something "they'll never forget you said one time"—and, even after they tell you what it was, you can't remember saying it? A dear brother once told me I had shaped his understanding of the local church more than anyone else. I was encouraged, but also humbled because *I couldn't remember a single time I had intentionally taught him anything about the church.* He's now a faithful pastor in Illinois. I hadn't counted our conversations as all that important. But cumulatively, they shaped his view of and affection for the church.

Now, again, stack up those uncounted conversations across the weeks and months and years. How much good has been done by your words that you don't even know about?

Of course, most Christian conversations don't contain life-changing wisdom. But every Christian conversation *does* convey an example of how fellow Christians view the world (for good or ill!). The way that single sister responds to the children interrupting her "adult conversation"; the way that man speaks gently but sternly to another brother; the way that couple mention in passing that they've been struggling with arguing a lot lately—all these provide a fleeting but vivid image of Christian faithfulness.

Such interactions function as tiny course corrections as you drive down a long, straight highway. Many of them don't even register on your consciousness. But thank goodness you make them. Individually, they don't count for much. But cumulatively, they keep you on the straight and narrow.

Once you recognize the value of mundane conversations like these, their significance increases. You'll begin to utilize your own passing conversations with greater intentionality.

What do you choose to talk about after the corporate gathering? As long as I've known him, my friend Brinton has consistently turned to whoever's next to him and asked them what edified them from the sermon they just heard. What a simple and obvious thing to talk about after church! He's done this for nearly twenty years. I wonder how much good that simple question has done.

I've mainly referred here to those conversations that happen around a congregation's corporate worship. Obviously, the same principle holds the other six days in a week. But the conversations around our corporate gatherings are especially useful. This is, after all, the time and place with the most opportunity.

Perhaps I should have started with this. But I'm convinced these kinds of intentional conversations are commanded of us in Scripture. Hebrews 10:23–25 exhorts us not to neglect meeting together as is the habit of some, but encouraging one another. And how are we meant to encourage each other? By meeting together, and by stirring one another up to love and good works.

That happens in our formal worship, yes. But we also stir one another up in those conversations on the way out the door. Christian conversation is the most overlooked conveyer of Christian doctrine and Christian ethics. It's often the means by which believers better understand the implications of the Word they've just sat under.

CONCLUSION

Raising up believers to maturity in Christ is a daunting task. It's only possible due to the Spirit's enlivening and sanctifying work. But beloved, be encouraged in the task. The Lord uses more than the scheduled events, the carefully planned sessions, and the lovingly crafted sermons. He's also ordained ordinary Christian speech as a means to maturity in Christ.

Consider Ephesians 4:15–16. How do grow up in every way into him who is the head? How are we to be joined, united, and equipped by our Savior? How might we help the rest of the body build itself up in love? By "speaking the truth in love."

Now go and do likewise.

ABOUT THE AUTHOR

Caleb Greggsen pastors an English-speaking church in Central Asia.

Between Sundays: Life in the Means of Grace

Raymond Johnson

SUNDAY

With ten minutes to spare, David sat down in the pew that had become his usual spot—the top right balcony. He looked up to see Dan, a friend whose wife recently left him. It was messy, and news of his wife's affair had made its way through the congregation even as the elders prayed and worked behind the scenes to help. David quickly prayed for Dan: "Father, I cannot imagine what Dan feels at every moment of every day, but I remember the verse I read yesterday morning that said that we have a merciful and faithful High Priest in the Lord Jesus. Please help him know that you are touched by the feelings of our infirmities. Help him to know you are not distant, but near during this time of horrific suffering."

The service began with the usual Call to Worship. David remembered the text from Psalm 95:1: "Oh come, let us sing to the Lord; let us make a joyful noise to the rock of our salvation!" Honestly, he didn't feel like singing, or really even being there. Last week had been a hard week. His presentation before the management team hadn't gone well, and there was talk he might not be a good fit for his job. And yet, when he heard the presiding minister read the words, "the rock of our salvation," his mind began to focus on those words. He needed a rock at the moment, and the salvation he had heard about since his childhood was becoming more and more valuable to him. "Salvation," the pastor stated from the pulpit, "is our greatest need, and God has done for us what we could not do for ourselves."

"Right now, I feel like I can do nothing for myself," David thought. Then came the opening hymn: "Come We That Love the Lord." It spoke of "marching to Zion, the beautiful city of God." This was one of David's favorite hymns from childhood, and today, the words, "We're marching through Immanuel's ground to fairer worlds on high" helped him remember that no matter what he faced last week or would face this week, the Lord Jesus himself had walked on earth and lived perfectly, died vicariously, and rose victoriously for him. Slowly his mind focused on the words of the Bible, and when he prayed, he began to pour out his heart to God.

A verse came to his mind as he began to pray with the minister: "Trust in him at all times, O people; pour out your heart before him; God is a refuge for us." David began to pour out his heart to God in prayer. He remembered how he slandered his friend, Michael, who had slandered him. He asked God to forgive him; he knew he should be praying for those who were standing against him at work. Slowly, with each mention of his sin, he grew simultaneously more concerned and more comforted. The more he thought, the more sin he remembered. The more sin he remembered, the more he worried about his soul. When he heard the words from the minister promising God's forgiveness, he thought, "I have no hope because I can't stop sinning—at least in this life."

The sermon focused on Romans 5:1–11. It was a difficult passage to understand, but as the pastor explained what it meant to stand justified by faith and to stand in the grace of God, even through trials and sufferings, a confidence in God slowly grew in his heart. "God is building something in me," David thought. "Even though it's hard, and I hate all I'm going through at work, I know the Lord has promised to never waste trials. He uses them to change me and make me more holy."

MONDAY

David was up early on Monday morning to exercise. As he jogged, he listened to Scripture. This morning it was hard to concentrate because he didn't want to face everyone in the office. It felt as if everyone was against him because of what happened last week. "Do not be anxious about anything, but in everything by prayer and supplication with thanksgiving let your requests be made known to God." This was the verse that stuck with him from his morning Scripture reading podcast. "Father," David prayed, "I am scared about what might happen, but I ask that you help me in everything I will face today."

By the time he walked into the office, he saw his boss coming down the hall. His heart fell and dread overtook him. Suddenly this hymn came to mind: "Fear not, I am with thee, O be not dismayed, for I am Thy God and will still give thee aid." He took a deep breath and walked on. His boss greeted him and said to him that he would be working with him to get things more on track.

David immediately thought, "I am terrible at this job and really terrible at everything I do." Suddenly, these thoughts drove him into sadness. Three weeks ago, the assistant pastor preached a sermon on prayer and speaking truth to ourselves by the power of the Holy Spirit. "Father, I am really scared and feel terrible at the moment. I worry life is about to fall apart, and then I will be all alone and not know what to do." As he prayed, he began to realize that no matter what happened, God was in control of his life.

Last week his best friend, James, reminded him that the pain of his past didn't have to keep affecting him every day. More talking, praying, and simply applying the truth of Scripture helped him to arrest bad thoughts before they took over his mind and sent him down a path of despair.

WEDNESDAY

As the week progressed, each day seemed to get a little easier. David's routine helped him stay on track spiritually and at work. Wednesday night, after mid-week Bible Study, he had his weekly dinner with James from church. This was his favorite time of the week because when they got together, they always talked about the Lord and encouraged each other. Somewhere between laughing and walking and eating, David's loneliness drifted away.

FRIDAY

During his devotions on Friday, David glanced at the upcoming order of worship online and noticed the congregation would be observing the Lord's Supper. As he took a few moments to reflect on the table, he recalled that though he had asked God to forgive him for slandering Michael, he had not yet reconciled personally with him. He felt like he couldn't approach the table in good conscience. So he texted him to set up a meeting. After reading Jesus' teaching in the Sermon on the Mount, he took courage and was resolved to the task. Even though confessing his sin to Michael was humiliating in the moment, the forgiveness and reconciliation he received ended up being life-giving for his soul.

SATURDAY

Saturday, he reflected on Friday's conversation with Michael, he recalled the joy he felt when he witnessed Michael's baptism, and the thankfulness that his profession of faith meant he was a genuine brother in Christ. Those memories reminded David of the unity of the Spirit in the bond of peace he now shared with the rest of his congregation, leading him to strategize how he might do spiritual good tomorrow for other members of his church.

SUNDAY (AGAIN)

By the time Sunday returned, David found himself in the same place—the top right balcony. The service began, and all the familiarity reminded him of the foundation for his trust in God. David hadn't missed a worship service in about six months. His life had become bound up with the people and the work of the gospel at work in this church. Week by week. Sunday by Sunday. Their pastor had taught them through the "ordinary means of grace."

"Blessed is the man who walks not in the counsel of the wicked, nor stands in the way of sinners, nor sits in the seat of scoffers, but his delight is in the law of the Lord, and on his law he meditates day and night." The service began with these words. The sheer predictability of the next 90 minutes was the opposite of boring. Instead, the words of Scripture and the songs of the saints and the sermon from his pastor worked to transform his heart, *their* hearts.

"I can't live without these words and this place," David thought.

ABOUT THE AUTHOR

Raymond Johnson is the senior pastor of Christ Church West Chester in West Chester, Pennsylvania.

The Freedom that Comes from Being Boringly Biblical

Eric Bancroft

"*Come see my naked pastor.*"

This was what the banner along the highway said. As people came home from work, dropped their kids off at soccer practice, ran to the grocery store, or went to see their *abuelas* on the weekend, they were being wooed by a local church. The draw? Apparently, this church employed a naked man as their pastor. The provocative sign promoted a new sermon series during which the pastor would be honest about his life and the challenges he had faced. This was supposed to help people relate to him and by association, the church, so they would feel comfortable and want to come back.

I wish I could tell you that this is a fictitious story. After all, aren't pastors known for their made-up illustrations? But it's true.

While this story might push the envelope for most outreach-oriented progressives, it nevertheless demonstrates how far some churches and their leaders are willing to go to "reach" people. From the promise of live animals on nativity sets, to helicopter Easter Egg drops, to free iPads, some churches pull out all the stops to make invitations difficult to deny.

You might wonder, aren't such efforts good? After all, the church is called to be committed to outreach.

NOT SO FAST

Before you sign up for another conference promising a double portion of outreach blessing or beat yourself up for not being as creative as other churches around you, stop and ask some fundamental questions. What does God want your church services to look like? Can it fundamentally be reduced to outreach, or should we be mindful of other priorities? Are you, as a pastor, called to be the Chief Avant-Garde Officer? Or are you called to be a shepherd who must give an account to God for those he has put under your care?

We need to remember that the visible church is a gathering of Christians in a local assembly to worship the Lord. No longer offering animals on altars, we offer our lives as living sacrifices to our great God and King who loved us even while we were yet sinners and sent his Son to die for us (Romans 12:2; 5:8). We gather first and foremost to worship God for redeeming us in Christ. Problems will arise in our gatherings if we turn our gaze away from the risen Savior to the lost sinner. At best, we'll be distracted. At worst, we'll distort the bride of Christ who is being prepared for his return (Revelation 19:7).

This doesn't mean we should ignore the non-Christians in our gatherings, nor should we invite them to come (1 Corinthians 14:23). But pastors, we would do well to renew our vows to our calling, namely "to equip the saints for the work of ministry, for building up the body of Christ" (Ephesians 4:12). We are not called to lead a technique-based, gimmick-oriented, and sensory-driven church with all the candles and fragrance dispensers our allergies can handle. We are called to lead our churches with the ordinary means of grace, namely the Word, prayer, and the ordinances of baptism and the Lord's Supper. We sing songs of lament because we know firsthand the effects of a sinful world, and we sing songs of praise as we take comfort in a triumphant and sovereign God who is working all things together for our good and his glory (Romans 8:28).

Is this a call to a boring, lifeless gathering? By no means! It's a call to the full range of human experience. It takes into account the revelation God has given us through his Word.

WHERE DID ALL THE BIBLES GO?

Thankfully, our decoding of Instagram algorithms, our pioneering work on Tik-Tok, or our streaming content on Twitch will not be the secret-sauce we build upon. Our churches should instead bank our hope on the undiluted proclamation of God's Word by undistracted pastors (2 Timothy 4:2). God's Word is powerful, sharper than any two-edged sword (Hebrews 4:12).

Pastors, do you believe this?

Here's a test for us this coming Sunday: How much will your people need their Bibles to understand and navigate what is being sung, read, prayed, or taught to them? Will there be a "hat-tip" to the Creator and a passing citation of his Word? Is the preaching marked by emotion more than exposition, by culturally savvy one-liners more than targeted application? Or will you carve up the meat of God's Word so much so that people need "doggy bags" to take it home? Will their hearts be full God's Word sung, prayed, read, and preached? Will they have much to ponder themselves and talk about with others in the days ahead, both Christians and non-Christians?

TO GOD BE THE GLORY

One of my neighbors runs a small circus company (think a mini-me version of Cirque du Soleil). When he learned I was a pastor, he let me know that one of his clients was a local church that hired his company to come in and be a part of their sermon series, trapeze artists and all. I found myself at a loss of words. I wanted to express my appreciation that his company was doing well financially, but I was also sad to hear about a church who was supposed to be the pillar and buttress of truth resorting to such gimmicks (1 Timothy 3:15).

Pastor, there's freedom in a simple philosophy of ministry.

God hasn't called you to creativity, or outpacing expectations. He's called you to a ministry of proclamation where you preach God's Word without reservation or hesitation. He's called you to a ministry of shepherding, and he's told you that you will give an account to God for the lives he has entrusted to you. He's called you to a ministry of intercession, in which you ask for God's will to be done in the lives of his people.

Whether in private counseling or public proclamation, pastors are called to put the glories of Christ before their people even as the tragedies of this world and the sin in their hearts try to trick them to believe the lies of the Evil One. Pastor, you are called to preach and pastor, shepherd and model, love and forgive. You're called to remind them of the faith they articulated at their public baptism, and to renew that faith by regularly coming to the Lord's table.

That's your job description. Read it again, and then go to bed and sleep well. Rest in the truth that you have been faithful to what the Lord has called you to do today. Let God be God. Whatever he brings from your labor is his doing—and it is all of grace.

ABOUT THE AUTHOR

Eric Bancroft is the pastor of Grace Church, a new church in Miami, Florida.

"The Word Did It All": The Necessity of Preaching According to the Protestant Reformers

Shawn Wright

One danger of being familiar with history is just that. It becomes familiar to us. Or so we think. Our familiarity with the facts, the cause-effect relationships, and the narrative may keep us from actually seeing what happened, or why what took place matters for us. The narrative of the Protestant Reformation serves as a case in point. Martin Luther (1483–1546) simply read the Bible, rediscovered the doctrine of justification by faith alone (*sola fide*), and preached the gospel. And in the process, he and later Reformers like John Calvin (1509–64) turned the world upside down.[1] Right?

1 Michael Reeves winsomely presents the narrative of the Protestant Reformation in *Unquenchable Flame: Discovering the Heart of the Reformation* (Nashville, TN: B&H, 2010). A fuller treatment that acknowledges the religious and doctrinal focus is Carter Lindberg, *The European Reformations*, 2nd ed. (Malden, MA: Wiley-Blackwell, 2009).

Not so fast, argues Brad Gregory. Gregory, a highly trained Reformation historian, argues that the Reformation unbound the tightly-knit-together world of the Thomistic synthesis between faith and reason and the Catholic conception of Christendom in which secular and religious cohered closely together. Unknowingly, Luther unleashed a torrent that swelled into the modern world with all its post-Enlightenment problems.

In other words, the Protestant reformers unwittingly caused modernity. How? Most fundamentally by turning away from the Catholic church's definition of dogma to the view that the Bible, not the church, determined the truth. *Sola scriptura* caused the problems the West has faced in modernity.[2]

2 For Gregory's extended argument see Brad S. Gregory, *The Unintended Reformation: How a Religious Revolution Secularized Society* (Harvard, MA: Harvard University Press, 2012). He highlights the negative effects of *sola scriptura* in "A Response to Evangelicalism" in *Journeys of Faith: Evangelicalism, Eastern Orthodoxy, Catholicism, and Anglicanism*, ed. Robert L. Plummer (Grand Rapids, MI: Zondervan, 2012), 165–178. Readers might be interested in two insightful reviews of Gregory's argument, the first by Michael Horton (https://www.thegospelcoalition.org/reviews/the-unintended-reformation/), the second by Carl Trueman (https://www.reformation21.org/articles/pay-no-attention-to-that-man-behind-the-curtain-roman-catholic-history-and-the-e.php).

LUTHER ON PREACHING AND PRAYER

When Luther and Calvin, though, described what led to the earth-shattering transformations of their days, with one voice they declared the recovery of the gospel and the clear preaching of that gospel which caused people to come out of spiritual darkness into light. *Sola fide* flowed from *sola scriptura*.

Luther struggled for months (or longer!) to understand how "the righteousness of God" (which he thought *must* refer to God's retributive justice) could be "good news" in Romans 1:16–17. After finally seeing that God graciously imputed Christ's righteousness to his people,[3] Luther described the doctrine of justification by faith alone as "the summary of all Christian doctrine" and "the article by which the church stands or falls." [4]In another place he observed, "Nothing in this article [of justification] can be given up or compromised, even if

3 See Martin Luther, "Two Kinds of Righteousness," in *Martin Luther's Basic Theological Writings*, ed. Timothy F. Lull (Minneapolis, MN: Fortress, 1989), 155–164.
4 Timothy George, *Theology of the Reformers* (Nashville, TN: Broadman, 1988) 62.

heaven and earth and things temporal should be destroyed ... On this article rests all that we teach and practice against the pope, the devil, and the world."[5]

Luther argued that the tide of the Reformation swept forward on the preaching of the Word of God alone: "I simply taught, preached, wrote God's Word; otherwise I did nothing. And then, while I slept, or drank Wittenberg beer . . . the Word so greatly weakened the papacy that never a prince or emperor did such damage to it. I did nothing. The Word did it all."[6]

There you have it. The Word did it all.

In order for the church to gather as the people of God, there must be both the preaching of the Word of God and prayer, Luther exhorted. "At each service a passage of Scripture is to be read and then interpreted. This is to be followed by the praying of the Psalms and other prayers." [7]Luther stressed that the Word was the very Word of Christ. And Christ brought the Word to bear with power by means of his Spirit. Although "God uses the ordinary means of the reading and preaching of the Word by ministers of the gospel," nonetheless the Word "becomes inward when inwardly it is received and believed. This is the work of the Holy Spirit. It is through the Word that the Holy Spirit works."[8]

CALVIN ON PREACHING AND PRAYER

Calvin agreed with Luther the pioneer. He described justification by faith alone as "the main hinge on which religion turns."[9] And the means of proclaiming this exquisite gospel is the ordinary preaching of the Word of God. Calvin counted it "a singular privilege" that God had consecrated "to himself the mouths and tongues of men in order that his voice may resound in them."[10] Preaching is essential. In fact, nothing is "more notable or glorious

5 Martin Luther, *The Smalcald Articles*, in *Martin Luther's Basic Theological Writings*, 502–503.

6 George, *Theology of the Reformers*, 53.

7 Hughes Oliphant Old, *The Reading and Preaching of the Scriptures in the Worship of the Christian Church. Vol. 4: The Age of the Reformation* (Grand Rapids, MI: Eerdmans, 2002), 31.

8 Old, *Reading and Preaching of the Scriptures*, 41.

9 John Calvin, *Institutes of the Christian Religion*, Library of Christian Classics, 2 volumes, ed. John T. McNeill, trans. Ford Lewis Battles (Philadelphia: Westminster, 1960), 3.11.1.

10 Calvin, *Institutes*, 4.1.5.

in the church than the ministry of the gospel, since it is the administration of the Spirit and of righteousness and of eternal life."[11]

And Calvin lived as he wrote. He preached—a lot! John Leith's comment is apt, and understated: "The sheer volume of Calvin's preaching is impressive." Always conceiving of the regular preaching ministry as his primary calling, the Genevan pastor carried an impressive preaching load. For about the last 15 years of his life he preached twice on Sunday and once Monday through Saturday, on alternate weeks. Just from 1549 to 1560, he preached 2,042 sermons. According to Dawn DeVries, between 1541 and 1564 Calvin preached through "the Psalms, Jeremiah, Lamentations, Micah, Zephaniah, Joel, Amos, Obadiah, Jonah, Daniel, Ezekiel, 1 and 2 Thessalonians, 1 and 2 Timothy, Titus, 1 and 2 Corinthians, Job, Deuteronomy, Isaiah, Galatians, Ephesians, Harmony of the Gospels, Acts, Genesis, Judges, 1 and 2 Samuel, and 1 Kings." His output included 200 sermons on the book of Deuteronomy, 174 on Ezekiel, and 189 on Acts.[12] When the entire corpus of Calvin's sermons is considered, it constitutes nearly half of everything this prolific author wrote. Though Calvin preached with no notes, the Geneva city council knew what a phenom they had in Calvin. So they paid for a group of secretaries to take the preacher's sermons down and publish them.[13]

Why did Calvin dedicate so much time to preaching? Simply—and incredibly—because in it God communicated to his people: "When the Gospel is preached in the name of God, this is as much as if he himself did speak in his own person." Almighty God, who dwells in unapproachable light, communicates through the preaching of his Word. And he does so in such a way as to make the gospel go forth with power to save his elect:

The voice of man is nothing but a sound that vanishes in

11 Calvin, *Institutes*, 4.3.3.

12 Dawn DeVries, "Calvin's Preaching," in *The Cambridge Companion to John Calvin*, ed. Donald K. McKim (Cambridge: Cambridge University Press, 2004), 111.

13 John H. Leith, "Calvin's Doctrine of the Proclamation of the Word and Its Significance for Today," in *John Calvin and the Church: A Prism for Reform*, ed., Timothy George (Louisville, KY: Westminster/John Knox, 1990), 206–207.

the air, and notwithstanding it is the power of God to salvation to all believers (saith Saint Paul). When then God speaketh unto us, by the mouth of men, then he adjoins the inward grace of his Holy Spirit, to the end, that the doctrine be not unprofitable, but that it may bring forth fruit. See then how we hear the heavenly Father: that is to say, when he speaketh secretly unto us by his Holy Spirit, and then we come unto our Lord Jesus Christ.[14]

Calvin believed that God spoke to his people through the ordinary means of the preaching of his Word. Through the preached Word, God saved his people. Through the preached Word, he conformed them more and more to Christ because God "will have nothing preached in his name but that which will profit and edify."[15]

Another reason pushed Calvin to stress the regular preaching of God's Word: people were often led astray from the proper means of knowing God and his will. Catholics pointed people to the church. The libertines and fanatics looked to remarkable experiences. Both were flawed, Calvin said. We know God in his Word as the Holy Spirit—who authored the book—illumines us to understand his Word. Calvin avers, "by a kind of mutual bond the Lord has joined together the certainty of his Word and of his Spirit so that the perfect religion of the Word may abide in our minds when the Spirit, who causes us to contemplate God's face, shines; and that we in turn may embrace the Spirit with no fear of being deceived when we recognize him in his own image, namely, in the Word."[16]

Both Luther and Calvin believed that the recovery of the biblical gospel of justification by faith alone was essential if people were to be born again. At the same time, the preached gospel also caused growth in Christians. For in preaching, God by his Spirit spoke. And he acted. So Luther and Calvin simply studied, prayed, and preached—and wrote, and discipled, and led, and worked themselves almost to death. And

14 John Calvin, third sermon on Jacob and Esau, quoted in Leith, "Calvin's Doctrine of the Proclamation of the Word," 227, n. 31.

15 John Calvin, sermon on 2 Timothy 2:16–18, quoted in Leith, "Calvin's Doctrine of the Proclamation of the Word," 222.

16 Calvin, *Institutes*, 1.9.3.

God used these flawed, but committed men to turn the world upside down.

HOW REFORMATION PREACHING CHANGED THE WORLD

The German and Swiss Reformations—and the Lutheran and Calvinist movements they led to—convulsed the world in the sixteenth century. A quick glance at the effects of the Calvinist side of the Reformation demonstrates the manner in which the preached Word built up the church. Calvin preached, pastored, and discipled others.[17] Not only did this lead to growth in the church in Geneva, but it also resulted in the Genevan church sending out church planters into France.

The French were quite hostile to the Protestant faith, but nonetheless the Genevan missionaries faithfully got to work. Before 1555, there doesn't seem to have been any organized effort on Geneva's part. But then they began sending young men—a lot of them. As Robert Kingdon recounts, "Between 1555 and 1563 the 'Register of the Company of Pastors' records some 88 missionaries sent, but this is only a partial number for the registers are incomplete."[18] What happened from the faithful preaching of these young men is remarkable. According to Pierre Courthial, "In 1555 there were five organized Reformed churches in France; in 1559, the year the first national synod assembled in Paris, there were nearly 100; and by 1562 they numbered 2,150."[19] The preached Word led to extraordinary growth through conversions and church-planting.

We could recount the manner in which the preached Word led to new life and spiritual depth in the Puritan era in England in the seventeenth century. We could also look to the way that preaching shook the English colonies in the First Great Awakening of about 1735 to 1745, fueled by Jonathan

17 A wonderful book on Calvin's pastoral ministry and that of the next generation is Scott M. Manetsch, *Calvin's Company of Pastors: Pastoral Care and the Emerging Reformed Church, 1536–1609* (Oxford: Oxford University Press, 2012).

18 Robert M. Kingdon, *Geneva and the Coming of the Wars of Religion in France, 1555–1563* (Geneva: Librarie E. Droz, 1956), 14.

19 Pierre Courthial, "The Golden Age of Calvinism in France," in *John Calvin: His Influence in the Western World*, ed. W. Stanford Reid (Grand Rapids, MI: Zondervan, 1982), 77.

Edwards and George Whitefield. The common thread from the sixteenth to the eighteenth centuries was the faithful, clear, passionate preaching of God's Word *combined* with holding fast to the doctrine of justification by faith alone.[20]

20 On the growth of Calvinism, see Jon Balserak, *Calvinism: A Very Short Introduction* (Oxford: Oxford University Press, 2016), and John T. McNeill, *The History and Character of Calvinism* (Oxford: Oxford University Press, 1954). For Calvin's influence on missions, note Michael A. G. Haykin and C. Jeffrey Robinson, *To the Ends of the Earth: Calvin's Missional Vision and Legacy* (Wheaton, IL: Crossway, 2014).

CONCLUSION

God by his Spirit continues to work in the same way today. The Lord blesses the same gospel, and the same ordinary preachers who trust the authority of his Word and the necessity of the Holy Spirit to bring conviction and illumination.

In the Reformation, the Word did it all. Five hundred years from now, may that be said of your ministry and mine.

ABOUT THE AUTHOR

Shawn Wright is an Associate Professor of Church History at The Southern Baptist Theological Seminary in Louisville, Kentucky. He is also the Pastor of Leadership Development at Clifton Baptist Church.

Made in the USA
Columbia, SC
03 August 2021